AF876500

CRITICAL ISSUES IN CARIBBEAN DEVELOPMENT

Number 6

Elements of Regional Integration: The Way Forward

CRITICAL ISSUES IN CARIBBEAN DEVELOPMENT

Number 1 West Indian Development and the Deepening and Widening of the Caribbean Community
William Demas

Number 2 The New World Trade Order: Uruguay Round Agreements and Implications for CARICOM States
Frank Rampersad et al

Number 3 Institutional Aspects of West Indian Development
Jones, Mills, Clarke, Brown, Le Franc, Henry

Number 4 Jamaica After NAFTA: Trade Options and Sectoral Strategies
Usha Viswanathan and Ann Weston, eds.

Number 5 Jamaica's Export Economy: Towards a Strategy of Export-led Growth
Donald J. Harris

Number 6 Elements of Regional Integration: The Way Forward
Wickham, Duncan, Wedderburn, Antrobus & Andaiye, Serbin, Jácome, Augustus

CRITICAL ISSUES IN CARIBBEAN DEVELOPMENT

Number 6

Elements of Regional Integration: The Way Forward

Peter Wickham
Neville Duncan
Judith Wedderburn
Peggy Antrobus & Andaiye
Andrés Serbin
Francine Jácome
Kertist Augustus

IRP
Ian Randle Publishers
Kingston, Jamaica
and
Caribbean Policy Development Centre
Barbados

Published in Jamaica 1998 by
Ian Randle Publishers
206 Old Hope Road, Box 686
Kingston 6, Jamaica, W.I.

in association with the

Caribbean Policy Development Centre
Barbados

© Caribbean Policy Development Centre

All rights reserved–no part of this publication may be reproduced, stored in a retrieval system, or transmitted in any form, or by any means electronic, photocopying, recording or otherwise without the prior permission of the author or publisher.

ISBN 976-8123-75-3

A catalogue record for this book is available from
The National Library of Jamaica.

Cover and book design by Kathryn Daniel, Southpaw Grafix

Set in 10/13 ITC Garamond x 27

Printed and bound in the U.S.A.

Contents

Introduction

The idea that there are benefits in unity for Caribbean and indeed all American people is not new. Simón Bolivar (1783-1830) 'El Libertador', the leader of revolt of South American colonies against Spanish rule, is regarded as the father of the Pan American vision.

Bolivar founded Grand Colombia comprising what are now Venezuela, Colombia, Panama and Ecuador, a union from which Venezuela was the first to withdraw.

Bolivar's vision would have found support from the fledgling US power that was espousing the 'Monroe Doctrine' of 1823, which articulated a principle of US policy declining any European intervention in the political affairs of the American continent.

This vision of the hemisphere - homogeneous even in its diversity - was largely promulgated at the level of governmental and political actors. In the history of humanity, this visionary approach to superseding national frontiers is not revolutionary. Expansion for reasons of trade and other means of survival or merely for glory is spread across history.

In the Anglophone Caribbean, the early attempts at integration, if it might be so regarded, were of necessity proposed by the colonial power. As Augier and Gordon noted in their 'Sources of West Indian History' (p. 252): 'In the eighteen-thirties the British Government adopted the policy of reducing the number of separate governments in the West Indies whenever possible. This policy was not accepted by the West Indians who were in politics, and throughout the nineteenth century, although the British Government made attempts to execute the policy, little was accomplished.'

There was the suggestion that integration would bring social benefits to the colonies as correspondence in 1831 from the Secretary of State to the Governor of British Guiana, cited by Augier and Gordon, shows.

An 1873 attempt by the Secretary of State to sell the benefits of federation among the Leewards in order to induce Barbados and the Windwards to federate, aroused only 'suspicion and jealousy' in the islands. The Barbados House of Assembly rejected the idea and some planters told their workers that federation would mean a return to slavery. The ensuing 'Confederation Riots' in Barbados in 1876 put paid to the notion.

Vested interest might have prevailed in those early attempts but did not dampen a spirit that existed in a burgeoning movement that saw solutions to common problems through cooperation. Workers, professionals, small farmer bodies and pressure groups coalesced into a political movement that often looked beyond territorial boundaries. For example, by 1917, Grenada's Marryshow was urging Trinidadians to support Grenadians in a demand for representative government.

While that early movement, after much trial and tribulation, culminated in the Federation of the West Indies in 1958, that government which combined 10 islands lasted only until 1962, falling under the pressure of political opportunism. The members eventually gained separate political independence from Britain but with an atavistic trait for unity.

Outside the political sphere the flame of integration in the English-speaking Caribbean has been kept ablaze by institutions such as the West Indies cricket team which has survived more than half a century and attained world-beating status. And, as the contribution to this volume by Peggy Antrobus and Andaiye recalls, informal traders and cultural workers have kept the region eating mangoes, eddoes and farine while dancing to the same kaiso and reggae tunes.

The governments have maintained tangible commitment to the idea, too, even if many contend that fervour is lacking. This is evidenced in the presence of the Caribbean Community (CARICOM), the Organisation of Eastern Caribbean States (OECS), the University of the West Indies, the Caribbean Examinations Council, the Caribbean Agricultural Research and Development Institute and many other organs that emphasise functional cooperation. CARICOM was also the leading player in the establishment of the Association of Caribbean States (ACS) which envisions integration at the widest regional level.

Integration activities, meantime, continue apace around the globe. Europe's most recent journey towards unification seems to be propelled by a lust for a perpetual peace. It is ironic that bureaucrats are creating a borderless Europe for politicians who are building walls against Napoleons and Hitlers.

To much of the world outside Europe, M. Bonaparte and Herr Hitler have retreated to the boardrooms of corporate Europe. This is the challenge faced by Caribbean and Latin American integrationists. In a universe of dilemmas, governments must chose between sailing alone and be overwhelmed in an ocean of free trade or be subsumed into some regional regime that must be strong enough as a bloc to compete in the world of corporate governance.

Even with the collapse of the Soviet empire, the Marxian analysis does not lose significance. Are we witnessing the withering of the state? Is history still a progressive movement, and have state lines been drawn in the 'class war' - that is, the integrated poor South countries vs. the homogenised, wealthy, corporate North? And what of the Asian Tigers?

This book attempts to address many of the issues faced by the integration movement of the Caribbean basin embracing all cultural and ethnic groups. The writers are from the English- and Spanish-speaking countries; from the islands and from the mainland; from labour and academia and the women's movement. The works were either commissioned by the Caribbean Policy Development Centre (CPDC) or presented in fora which addressed the critical issues of governance, democracy and participation of the developmental non-governmental organisations (NGOs) and other civil sectors in the integration movement.

The vision that is presented does not advocate integration for its own sake but as a means of putting the advancement of people at the centre of development.

The book addresses the issues of action and reaction, recognising that integration is not only stimulated by urges from within but also emerges from the dialectic of globalisation.

Peter Wickham's article on 'recapturing popular sovereignty' assumes that the power of the state is being eroded, and that that power which is being lost disempowers the 'grass-roots' people from whom power flowed through participation in 'popular' activities like free and fair elections. Further, the pooling of sovereignties could arrest the crisis situation and re-empower the people, he argues. Wickham, like Dr. Neville Duncan, sees an important role for the NGO movement in attempts to attain integration and in the new order of governance needed for its attainment.

The current recognition of labour, business, developmental NGOs and other interest groups as 'social partners' by individual governments and the institutions of integration such as CARICOM and the ACS is credited by the authors. The Joint Consultative Group to CARICOM comprises labour represented by the Caribbean Congress of Labour, the private sector represented by the Caribbean Association of Industry of Commerce and NGOs of which the Caribbean Policy Development Centre (CPDC) is treated as the NGO representative. None of the writers foresee a dissolution of governments with the ascension of NGOs and other actors from civil society but they recognise the need for deeper accommodation in a partnership for good governance.

As Judith Wedderburn notes in her piece, institutions such as the World

Bank and other lending agencies are now aware of 'performance lapses of Caribbean governments'. At the same time, it is being recognised that developmental NGOs have been able to identify the real needs of people and form partnerships with community-based organisations to contribute to the development of meaningful programmes and projects.

The Latin contributors, Andrés Serbin and Francine Jácome delve more deeply into issues of democracy, governance and governability and it is important to note the denotative meanings of these two latter terms as used by the Spanish speakers. 'It is necessary to differentiate between the Anglo-Saxon term "governance" and the notion of governability in Spanish, as Tomassini points out,' notes Serbin, 'because the latter includes the former and refers to broader processes that include "authority's capacity to channel the interests of civil society, the interaction that emerges between both segments and, therefore the legitimacy of the first of these: the government." '

If much of the writing is academic, not so the contributions by Antrobus and Andaiye on gender issues in regional integration, and Kertist Augustus on the role of labour. These address nitty-gritty issues such as access to health care, culture, jobs and freedom of movement of the individual.

These seven articles capture the philosophical and mundane modalities of the integration movement. They do not speak of political union, monetary or customs union nor do they even remotely consider military strategising as Bolivar must have but they do provide in good measure fertile material for the intellectual strategists and the grass-roots activists for wider Caribbean integration.

Mark Lee
April 1998.

Foreword

The goal of regional cooperation and integration lies in the search for an improved quality of life for all the people of the Caribbean region; a search made even more urgent by the imperatives of globalisation. The people of the region support the general will for Caribbean unity and applaud the consultative process which aims to bring on board the broadest possible base of the community of Caribbean people. The efforts within the Organisation of Eastern Caribbean States (OECS) towards political unity and the courage and tenacity of the four Windward Islands in undertaking to get that process going commands admiration. These efforts constitute the nucleus of a long-term growth into unity which will eventually bring together the Dutch, English, French and Spanish speaking Caribbean.

It took much time and encouragement before Caribbean leaders decided to respond to our sisters and brothers in Haiti but we can feel comfortable about the Caribbean Community's (CARICOM's) role in accompanying the Haitian people in their search for the building of a new society. A sense of urgency was lacking in CARICOM's practical response to challenges of an erupting volcano faced by the people of Montserrat but we finally came through with more than just words. In the case of the Cooperative Republic of Guyana, its latest political crisis has met with a readier CARICOM response dramatising our capacity to find ways of demonstrating regional cooperation and integration without violating the republic's national sovereignty.

Despite these achievements, there is the question of freedom of movement. CARICOM has laboured with some success to promote the free movement of goods. We are still to achieve the free movement of people to trade, to access medical care, to share their cultural legacy, to work together on mutual interests or simply to know each other. It is a fact that certain CARICOM nationals are hassled by immigration and customs authorities as they attempt to move about their own region, and the English-speaking Caribbean remains limited to one main language of communication.

Commendable progress is being made towards the achievement of a single market and economy, and in formulating concerted responses to the international lending agencies and trade blocs; regional approach has held some pleasant surprises about our inherent strength.The people of the region have demonstrated in their family composition, trading habits, pursuit of education and training, cultural sharing and sporting commitments that they see themselves as one people.The governments of the region have only one route to travel.

CRITICAL ISSUES IN CARIBBEAN DEVELOPMENT

Number 6

Elements of Regional Integration: The Way Forward

Julius Corriette (left) of the Carib Territory participates in the meeting of the Caribbean Organisation of Indigenous People, held in the Carib Territory of the Commonwealth of Dominica, September 1996

Towards recapturing popular sovereignty in the Caribbean through integration

PETER WICKHAM

Peter Wickham is a Ph. D. candidate in the Department of Behavioural Science, UWI, St. Augustine. His research interest is in Caribbean Affairs with special emphasis on Caribbean electoral behaviour. He is currently writing a dissertation that examines the dynamics of regional integration in the post-Cold War era.

Introduction

Sovereignty, in the context of the Caribbean, is often assumed to be a direct by-product of independence and a necessary constituent to our understanding of the implications of statehood. It is a feature of both ancient and modern states that persons in the Caribbean presume to have retained along with our constitutions that regulate political and legal activity in a defined geographical locality. While such a strict definition of sovereignty cannot be challenged, it is important to establish what this characteristic implies, allowing us to verify its existence in the Caribbean. Azcuy (1995) suggests that 'sovereignty implies that no external conditions, or no subordination to any other power exist, except by legitimate consent within permissible limits set by the State,' a statement that communicates more of what tangible sovereignty needs to achieve than a formal definition. This definition alone, however, does not fully communicate a suitable understanding without an examination of the significance of the term legitimacy. Here, legitimacy appears not only to imply democracy, but goes further to suggest the necessity of 'social acceptance' (Bogdanor 1992, 333). Cumulatively therefore we can, for the purposes of the discourse to follow, assemble a definition of sovereignty that includes both formal-legal aspects, as well as popular support as necessary ingredients and this is the interpretation that will be employed herein.

Having established that some distance exists between formal sovereignty and what can be described as popular sovereignty, the intention of this investigation becomes clear. It will thus attempt to demonstrate the means by which popular sovereignty is being eroded in the Caribbean and furthermore to highlight the ways in which the integration of Caribbean countries can act to retard, or even reverse, this process of erosion. The approach employed in dealing with this issue of sovereignty assumes that any erosion of sovereignty is inherently negative and moreover linked to the continued impoverishment and underdevelopment of Caribbean countries. Some amount of support for this assumption can come from the region's inability to secure international support for indigenous programmes of development, or alternatively our reliance on externally defined programmes. However, such conjectures must appreciate the contribution of other factors to Caribbean underdevelopment not explored in this paper. This discourse will therefore specifically examine the impact of globalisation forces on the sovereignty of Caribbean people and discuss the ways in which Caribbean non-governmental organisations (NGOs) could help to consolidate public opinion among the countries and in so doing empower Caribbean people, hence furthering democracy, in an attempt to identify alternatives and indigenous development models.

To accomplish this task it is important to establish the impact, or types of impacts, that globalisation has had on the sovereignty of the Caribbean, or the extent to which globalisation forces have eroded sovereignty, or made Caribbean people subordinate to external powers. In so doing, the concept of globalisation will be fully explored and placed in its historical context. Thereafter, a case can be made for closer integration within the Caribbean to be identified as a mechanism by which popular sovereignty can be repatriated to the region. A critical aspect of this exercise would be a demonstration that the inclusion of NGO opinion represents an enhancement of democracy within Caribbean states. Here the type of integration being proposed, and the actual ways in which it is envisaged that it could help secure sovereignty, would be discussed along with the ideal regional organisation to coordinate such effort. Such action would cumulatively represent an alternative model for development with broad-based popular support. Finally, attention will be turned to the NGOs and their historical role in the integration processes. This review will not only highlight the limited role of NGOs hitherto but will also highlight structural constraints to the participation of NGOs in the process of integration, suggesting structural modifications to regional institutions that might be necessary in the future, if Caribbean integration is to be an effective developmental tool.

I. GLOBALISATION AND THE SOVEREIGNTY OF CARIBBEAN PEOPLE

Saxe-Fernández (1995, 24) identified globalisation as 'a magical term that explains everything, justifies everything and furthermore, serves to unburden guilty consciences (if they are any) suffering between personal convictions with respect to loyalty to one's country and selling out.' This statement adequately sums up the apparent hopelessness perceived by developing countries regarding an international trend that has bred global capitalism and established and legitimised liberalism as the proper ideological orientation for the entire world.

Globalisation is certainly not a new phenomenon, having manifested itself in the Caribbean with the arrival of Columbus in 1492. It has been characterised by the expansion of empires and direct control of peripheral colonies by a central colonising power. However, as the concept of colonisation became less fashionable, equally effective and more durable indirect control in the form of neo-colonialism supplanted colonial control. Hence globalisation has many variants both historically and currently. However, it is more important to understand the ways in which this phenomenon is subordinating the people of the Caribbean to external powers and the impact that this activity is having on their lives. This reality can be demonstrated by reference to the increasing irrelevance of the nation state, which gives a macro theoretical perspective of globalisation and also a closer examination of specific sectors in which the effects of globalisation have been greatest: trade, the ideological bias and structural adjustment.

I. [I] GLOBALISATION AND THE NATION STATE

Any examination of the nation state attempted in this era is largely becoming an academic exercise since the national unit of analysis is ceasing to be relevant (Underhill 1993, 20). The Global Political Economy (GPE) has become so intrusive that states cannot easily implement national policies without impacting on other independent states. Furthermore, the current arrangement of the GPE is such that while states may pretend to be in control of policies such as economic growth and the foreign debt, they have long ago been forced to surrender these policies to the vagaries of the international capitalist market (Strange 1986, 3)[1].

Alternatively, it can be argued that some of the more significant problems - such as the illicit drugs trade, AIDS and environmental pollution - facing all countries today, require regional action at minimum. The realm of international politics as a result, cannot be segregated from national politics.

Such increasing irrelevance of the national entity had received considerable support during the Cold War era and is even more relevant now that an almost physical barrier to global interaction has been removed. Our discourse must therefore appreciate, not only the interplay of levels of analysis, but furthermore that the GPE is now truly global.

Characteristically, both national and international politics would need to be redefined. National politics will now need to contemplate an array of impacts from the international economy, transnational corporations and NGOs, in addition to appreciating the limited ability of the unit to alter its own economic development, while having to appear to be responding to the sectors of its population from whence its power is derived. International politics would similarly now be influenced from a liberal unipolar ideological perspective, and needs also to contemplate the importance of non-governmental actors.

Globalisation has also prompted questions about the 'sovereign structure' of the 'liberal democratic' state and as a result deemed inapplicable theoretical paradigms employed to analyse these structures (Held and McGrew 1993, 264) giving rise to several policy issues. The content of national policy is one such that can be expected to shift considerably in addition to the ways in which the policy is to be pursued. Interpreted more widely, it can be expected that states affect one another and similarly are affected by the actions of each other (Parry 1993, 144). The heavy influence of international actions on local policy is well documented with reference to the General Agreement on Tariffs and Trade (GATT). The most recent Uruguay round embraced areas such as trade in services and agriculture previously excluded from the ambit of the agreement. Hence, these areas which were previously part of national policy will now be dominated by agreements reached at these international fora, but requiring local action to secure implementation. Parry here uses the inclusion of the dubious economic activity known as services to illustrate the reach of international agreements. The maintenance of an economic advantage in services is important for less developed countries (LDCs) since labour being the major input makes the sector less capital intensive than industrial development programmes. Hence the control of this area demands that efforts at the local and regional level be brought within the realm of international norms.

Campanella (1993) has noted that globalisation demands have had a dual effect on policy making depending on their situation in either the centre or periphery of the GPE. Developed nations like the US have liberalised local politics to take full advantage of the hegemonic potential offered by the trends in the GPE, while LDCs are increasingly oriented towards self preservation by attempting to prevent the decline of their unit, or to prevent the irrelevance of policy. As a result, LDCs can and have been paying attention to regional economic linkages that bolster sovereignty, but provide an economic base sufficient to facilitate the pursuit of various national policies boosting domestic welfare, which is itself the source of the policy makers' power. The Caribbean countries appear to have identified the North American Free Trade Area (NAFTA) as the regional economic association worthy of pursuit. Whether membership in this organisation is achieved directly or by way of joint action of CARICOM is still uncertain. However, policy within developing states is increasingly preoccupied with liberalisation and managing policy in conformity with global guidelines. Policies toward regionalism are therefore motivated by and framed around reactions to global trends, instead of evolving based on local demands.

Specific discussion of such an impediment to policy creativity is offered by Brown (1988), who focuses on the futility of national policies that attempt to regulate market indicators such as inflation. Here the financial adjustments of transnational corporations can undermine governmental action to stabilise or stimulate a local economy. Furthermore, such action can handicap a government's ability to implement social policies designed to assist vulnerable sections of the population (Brown 1988, 159). A typical component of programmes like this might prevent transnationally mobile sections of the population from shifting their investments or funds to avoid high taxes or fair wages.

The quiet emergence of the Internet (Net) as a means of global interaction has coincidentally occurred around the same time as the ending of the Cold War and raises questions concerning the impact of information on national policy. Here, issues raised previously concerning the role of the media have taken on a completely new and more exaggerated dimension, now that every single individual with access to the Net facilities has the power to reach millions of people world wide. Ionescu (1993) discussed the potential harm to parliamentary sovereignties from this type of revolution by contrasting the traditional bipolar relationship of the parliament and people with the current situation where the media has intervened in this relationship to influence the policy preference of leaders in a way which was not totally unbiased. This was shown to affect the democratic traditions and supremacy of parliament since power now comes, not from the people, but from the ability to influence that which the parliamentarian communicates to the people. In developing countries the underdeveloped state of interest groups and inability of citisens to seek out information for themselves exaggerate the role of the Press as the guardian of information. Hence, the power to reach people becomes the power to influence people and hence policy.

The evolution of the Net as a mode of communication and information in developing countries has caused leaders to become subjected to the above-mentioned phenomenon on a global level. Therefore, international perspectives are now able to influence, by way of information, in a mode that is often superior to the capacity of developing nations to react. Recent national events within the USA such as the Senate confirmation hearings of Judge Robert Bork and later the murder trial of Othneil J. (O.J.) Simpson, have exposed Caribbean people to a level of transparency within these systems unavailable in the region. As a result, pressures have already begun to mount upon regional governments to adopt similarly transparent policies. Unfortunately, however, the sise and historical structure of Caribbean societies cannot always accommodate such transparency in government and calls into question the structural bases of such societies. Development therefore is forced to contemplate such issues which are thrust with great priority upon regional agendas already dominated by more pressing socioeconomic concerns.

The increased importance of multinational corporations (MNCs) in national economies raises the issue debated by Ball and Levitt (Gilpin 1970, 49) of whether the nation state should retreat allowing the productive potentials of the MNC to pilot development, or should a strong nationalism be encouraged to counterbalance the generation of a counter culture from the presence of foreign companies. While an attempt will not be made here to answer that issue definitively, the debate presents an issue that must be addressed in light of the increase in sise and scope of MNCs characteristic of this era. The Levitt side of this debate, raised originally with respect to Canada, identifies the vulnerability of LDCs in relation to penetration by foreign MNCs and the development of non-indigenous cultures.

Neo-liberalists such as Ball suggest that the nation state can and should become an entity that merely facilitates MNC development and expansion. Ultimately, these theorists would envisage total replacement of the state apparatus by that of the MNC. In contradistinction Gilpin argues that, while MNCs are likely to gain a greater foothold especially in economic matters, their influence is likely to be as an agent of various host governments. Support for this position is advanced by reference to the emergence of regional blocs in the EU, Japan and various LDCs which attempt to neutralise the power of the MNC, a phenomenon that is largely of American origin (Gilpin 1970, 69).

Strange (1988, 23) raises implications of this retreat of the nation state, where liberalisation allows the market to become so powerful that it assumes the authority of government. In liberalised societies, like that of the US, the power of the market is a reality that is legitimised by the deregulated structure of government, while in centrally planned economies market operators are constrained by pervasive structures. This point alone speaks to the type of structural change necessitated by adopting liberal economic practices and highlights the structural differences of centrally planned states. It is more important, however, that these structures are not accidental, but the result of deliberate surrender or acquisition of power for various reasons. She suggests that these structural differences are a result of a delicate admixture of societal values namely wealth, order, justice and freedom. Hence liberalisation of a centrally planned economy inherently alters this delicate balance and would appear to give greater prominence to wealth since the removal of controls, of necessity, allows the innate human condition to flourish which is often not a public interest concern. In LDCs the underdeveloped state of various social sectors requires a disproportionate level of assistance and protection, while developed societies often have less critical social and welfare concerns. LDC governments may therefore properly wish to retain power to determine the prioritisation of societal values and would seem likely to lean towards the European Union (EU) model in this regard that attempts to neutralise some of the more deleterious effects of the market centered economy.

I. [II] TRADE

Because of our colonial association with what has now become the EU, trade in the (Anglophone) Caribbean was assisted considerably by the Lomé conventions that established a system of preferences for African Caribbean and Pacific (ACP) states under GATT. Later the US developed the Caribbean Basin Initiative (CBI) and Enterprise of the Americas Initiative (EAI) and these have been the major trading preference schemes under which the Caribbean has sought to develop its trade sectors. An analysis of these yields a great deal of information on how trends in international trade have retarded the ability of Caribbean states to pursue trade-based development schemes.

Duncan (1995) concluded that the Lomé conventions have cumulatively done little to substantially develop Caribbean trade. The ACP/EU regime has always been limited, insisting on a relatively high value added, hence confining ACP countries to exports of raw and semi-raw agricultural products. Since exports outside of the prescribed range of items attracted duties, the Caribbean has never been able to use these preferences as a mechanism to develop the potential of their export sector. ACP preferences have inadvertently created a high level of dependence by Caribbean countries for the absorption of their agricultural products and have discouraged the development of industries that might process such products into goods that might be more marketable internationally. In so doing the Caribbean countries have replaced their former political dependence on the EU by economic dependence on EU markets for survival.

Recently, the development of the EU has facilitated access by third countries that has further eroded any privileged position enjoyed by ACP states. With regard to bananas, the Caribbean is currently attempting to grapple with the loss of a guaranteed market, since the publication of the World Trade Organisation (WTO) ruling that the provision of a protected market in the EU violates open trading rules of the global trade accords. To be sure, the bananas example is likely to be applied to sugar eventually, in keeping with trends in global trade. Such action will result in the Caribbean being left with a high priced agricultural product that cannot realistically compete on the international market and will inevitably result in a significant loss of foreign exchange to affected countries.

Trade with the US has also been subject to special arrangements that have not yielded major benefits. The CBI, a Reagan initiative, was the first coordinated effort to offer the Caribbean economic assistance by developing trade, a policy that in theory has the potential to facilitate long-term development and economic prosperity to Caribbean countries. The CBI's duty free concessions to Caribbean goods with a value added as low as 25 per cent was also sound in theory, but benefits were mitigated by quotas and restrictions that excluded the products that the Caribbean desired most to trade.

The EAI of US President Bush purported to encourage economic development in the Caribbean around the three pillars of trade, investment and debt relief. Of these three, only the debt reduction plan was really new (Hosten-Craig 1992, 57). Essentially, the EAI embraced the CBI initiatives and arguably minimised its benefits by enlarging the number of countries eligible to profit by including the larger developing countries such as Brazil. These Latin American countries often also have lower wages, which make them more capable of exploiting the trade advantages of the CBI. The philosophy of the EAI was also more far-reaching and intrusive than that of the CBI and had the potential to impact on the chosen developmental path of a Caribbean country. Here, liberal economic policies, such as open trade practices were deemed necessary to extract EAI benefits and were often counter productive.

The development of a Caribbean trade sector, a vital source of foreign exchange to fund development, has not benefited from either of these schemes designed to maintain markets for agricultural products and raw materials, or to develop a productive sector in the region. In both cases, inbuilt mechanisms served to retard the efficacy of what were essentially two dissimilar programmes, the latter of which was designed to remedy deficiencies of the former. At any rate, as the WTO ruling on bananas has demonstrated, regional trading schemes and global conventions regulating trade are overtaking these specialised trade development programmes.

Caribbean policy makers have therefore been forced to turn their attention to one of the largest free trade areas existing today and are now preoccupied with the necessity of adjusting to NAFTA. NAFTA's economy is estimated at around US$6 trillion (Duncan 1995) and appears to offer the potential of larger markets for all members to exploit. That the total output of CARICOM economies (US$12 billion in 1990) amounted to only six per cent of Mexico's GDP, coupled with the higher value added criterion imposed by NAFTA, suggests that the Caribbean stands to lose both current and future market share in the US as a result of this agreement. Duncan (1995) values the current bilateral trading relationship between the Caribbean and the US at over US$21 billion per year, with US imports from the region amounting to some US$8.2 billion. The real value of this relationship, however, lies in the thousands of jobs that it supports in the Caribbean and the huge share of the region's cumulative GDP that US exports comprise. Any erosion of this market share is likely to cause widespread loss of jobs and social hardship in the Caribbean. Such erosion is a virtual certainty when one considers the huge advantage that Mexico has over most of the Caribbean in wages alone.

Duncan (1995) has suggested that GATT is for most countries of the south like a poisoned chalice, a comment that seems fair when one considers the implications of this agreement. The Uruguay round of GATT went further than any previous GATT negotiation and appeared to be encroaching on the sovereignty of states by virtue of its attempt to regulate services, intellectual property and investment and furthermore by refining integrated mechanisms to penalise violation of these and other areas of the agreement. Certainly, this agreement that preceded the WTO, now a veritable world trade government, has worked in concert with the previously discussed trade programmes to facilitate widespread breaches of the sovereignty of states and has paved the way for the recolonisation of the once decolonised Caribbean countries. The international acceptance of the GATT protocols, along with its insistence on liberalism and deterrence to protection, gives Caribbean countries little alternative but to structure their legislative programmes along the lines of GATT understandings.

Raghavan (1990) has observed that the inclusion of non-trade issues and areas under the umbrella of GATT has been the catalyst to the process of recolonisation in the Caribbean. In this instance, colonisation is being spearheaded by the transnational corporations which are in turn motivated by capital. In order for these entities to function effectively, the largest possible market is necessary and such will be provided by NAFTA and ultimately the Free Trade Area of the Americas (FTAA). While capital is the objective in this scenario, international power is a welcomed by-product that helps to secure continuity. The inability of Caribbean countries to develop their economies due to this exploitative relationship with transnational corporations and the first world, is also a feature of the recolonisation process. Here, inappropriately designed foreign aid programmes, discussed above, have served only to create dependency and ultimately lead Caribbean countries towards international lending agencies with their commensurate conditionalities. Without even referring to the role of conditionalities with the lending agencies we can see that the function of trade agreements has been to impose a direction in development - or more appropriately, underdevelopment - that is conceived externally of the state and is likely to further subjugate it to foreign powers, a clear violation of the sovereignty concept.

I. [III] IDEOLOGICAL BIAS

The ideology behind the trade arrangements discussed above conveys a great deal about the process of globalisation currently being experienced and suggests further expected dimensions of this global process. It has its origins in the ending of World War II and the post war environment that emphasised the virtues of laissez faire economics. Hence, the financial support network for Caribbean countries, originating in and legitimised by the UN, created an appropriate international environment for transnationalisation to flourish. During this era the constraint on the global adoption of liberalism was the continuation of the Cold War and the pervasive ideological bipolarity. The ending of this ideological conflict, resulting in what has essentially been a victory by the US, has created an ideological unipolarity supporting neo-liberalism, with ample virgin territory to prevail upon. Hence neo-liberalism, nurtured in the post war period and based in a solid economic system, has become globalised with attendant implications for the economic wellbeing of Caribbean states.

The adoption of neo-liberal policies does not, in and of itself, compromise the sovereignty of Caribbean states. The problem instead stems from the forced imposition and continued pursuit of policies attendant to neo-liberalism that have simply not been in the best interest of Caribbean countries. Incontrovertibly, liberalism has not proven itself as a vehicle to 'economic plenty and social justice' (Watson 1994, 225) in the Caribbean. To demonstrate this, one needs only point to the experience of Jamaica. Here several studies (LeFranc 1994; Girvan et al 1990; Levitt 1991) have pointed to the severe economic and social hardships resulting from Jamaica's adoption of liberalism in the 1980s, which was itself a response to the apparent failure of socialism. Payne (1993, 28-53) draws a correlation between the failure of liberalism and the electoral defeat of the Jamaica Labour Party (JLP) that introduced this approach. Continued pursuit of the policies of liberalism notwithstanding suggests that an entity external to the Jamaican population is in a position to keep such programmes on the agenda, even if the result is the demise of a particular government.

The full impact that the exportation of neo-liberalism has had on sovereignty is probably best described with reference to the Helms-Burton Act that attempts to 'persuade' Cuba to adopt more liberal economic and political arrangements. The bill intends to tighten a long-standing economic embargo against Cuba by the US and employs special mechanisms to provide civil remedies to US citisens who have expropriation claims against the Cuban government. The titles of the bill (Titles III and IV) that deal with these claims run counter to the norms of international law since they attempt to provide a legal remedy in a second state, for acts committed in a first state where such acts were perfectly legal under the laws of that state. Implicitly Titles III and IV suggest that Cuba does not retain the competence to legislate on any and all matters within Cuba, based on the assumption that the Cuban politico-economic arrangement legitimising the government and inspiring the legislation is inherently wrong. Evidently, such a proposition suggests that issues of the Cuban government's legitimacy are better decided externally and attempts to violate all known notions of sovereignty.

The Helms-Burton Act also has serious trade implications for third countries that wish to trade with Cuba since companies in these countries could also find themselves subject to civil proceedings and visa restrictions, depending on the origins of their investments in Cuba. Hence the US is advertently influencing the ability of any company to trade with whomsoever they see fit. These concerns have caused the EU to lodge a complaint against the US with the WTO on the grounds that the bill will become a hindrance to the free flow of international trade, a proposition that seems quite logical. Ironically, the US made it known that it may not accept the ruling of the WTO, on the grounds that Helms-Burton legislation does not relate to international trade, but represents a concern of US national security. The veiled suggestion here is that the US should oppose threats to its national sovereignty and security, even if this represents a violation of another country's right to self-determination.

David Jessop (Trinidad Express, 27 Feb. 1997) notes that the Helms-Burton issue before the WTO represents a conflict of unilateralism being practised by the US against multilateralism that is otherwise encouraged by the US and upon which international trade and the WTO is premised. Such a contradiction is indicative of an ideological sanctimoniousness that justifies the transgression of long-standing norms of trade and international law by the US on any grounds. Similar thinking, no doubt, has been applied to the Shiprider.

The Agreement represents the most flagrant example of a bilateral agreement which, by its very suggestion, demonstrates little respect for the norms of international law and national sovereignty. Notwithstanding the noble basis of the agreement, designed to allow US authorities in hot pursuit of drug traffickers to continue such pursuits into the territorial waters of a signatory state without a Shiprider aboard, the proposal clearly represents an anomaly in international law. While Barbados and Jamaica identified the agreement as a violation of their national sovereignty, Trinidad and Tobago more quickly signed citing the activities of drug lords as a greater threat to Trinidad and Tobago's sovereignty than any 'outmoded' (Sunday Express, March 2, 1997) concept of sovereignty. Furthermore Trinidad and Tobago has suggested that the agreement pools the sovereignties of Trinidad and Tobago and the United States in this area and in so doing bolsters the sovereignty of the former country.

The fact that Trinidad and Tobago has not disagreed that the agreement represents a violation of sovereignty, but redefined the concept as being offset against such security concerns, demonstrates the fact that in our global community powerful states can easily construe issues to ensure that sovereignty becomes a lesser concern.

I. [IV] STRUCTURAL ADJUSTMENT

Caribbean structural adjustment programmes easily represent the best known facilitator of national sovereignty violations. These are well known and have been necessitated by the declining economic fortunes of Caribbean counties in the post-independence period reflected in widening balance of payments deficits. This shortfall was caused by the inability of former colonies to produce manufactured goods and the inadequacy of revenue from the export of raw materials to finance such purchases (McAfee 1991, 70). The IMF strategy of that time anticipated that these shortfalls would have been temporary, as raw materials' revenue was expected to rise and be assisted by the development of an export market for manufactured commodities in the region.

The Caribbean therefore drew heavily on the resources of various multilateral financial institutions (MFIs), as well as the very liquid private banking sector with this expectation in mind. By the end of the '70s it became clear that the rise in the cost of manufactured imports was far too steep to be met by the declining cost of raw material sales. As the situation threatened the existence of these institutions and the stability of the global economy, structural adjustment emerged that linked the refinancing of old debts to the attainment of systematic reductions in balance of payment deficits. In so doing, the IMF and World Bank, being the leading structural adjustment agencies, assisted the commercial banks in recovering some proportion of money - which continued to accrue high levels of interest - owed to them by debtor nations. A by-product of this refinancing method was, however, the introduction of conditionalities and controls where before no such intrusions existed.

The conditionalities attached to IMF/World Bank funding have been the traditional route to the erosion of sovereignty experienced by Caribbean countries. Here, in an effort to achieve balance of payments stability and, moreover, as a condition of accessing further funding, participating countries are required to take steps to reduce their balance of payments deficit which is one of the more general conditions. Additionally, domestic credit reductions are also required along with measures to liberalise trade and control government spending. Of the conditionalities, the latter two appear to affect a country's sovereignty more directly since there can be conflict with a preferred government policy to stimulate local industries by offering protection, or to use the public service as a tool of social engineering. Conditionalities instead impose a neo-liberal approach to trade and the structuring of the public service that may cause severe social hardship.

Ferguson (1995) has identified an even more intrusive development related to structural adjustment in the Caribbean and this is the association of governance issues with structural adjustment. Such an association has recently been gaining greater significance since the ending of the Cold War and the 'triumph' of the market driven economy and liberal forms of political democracy. The failure of alternative socialist models seems to have heralded the logic of adopting liberal democratic standards of governance as the paradigm that developing countries ought to work towards.

This thinking can be traced back to a World Bank study[2] relating to Sub-Saharan Africa which suggested that the failure of structural adjustment exercises had more to do with the political environment in which structural adjustment was approached. That necessary investment was discouraged by the 'unpredictability of policies... [and moreover]... uncertainty about their interpretation and application by officials' (World Bank 1989, 192). Such thinking therefore paved the way for lending agencies such as those involved in the process of structural adjustment to examine and involve themselves in the issue of governance, the specifics of which are defined by Ferguson as:

(i) how the people of a country are governed - the political dimension;

(ii) how the county's affairs are administered - the institutional dimension; and

(iii) the quality of management and institutional capacity to be found in public agencies - the technical dimension (Ferguson 1995, 161).

Over time the Multilateral lending agencies have assumed the task of supervising the institutional and technical dimensions of governance while bilateral donor governments have become involved in the political dimensions. Hence, the convergence of financial resources from bilateral donors is predicated on the quality of governance and uncooperative countries penalised by the withholding or discontinuation of aid (Robinson 1993).The donor community has therefore defined democratic governance and in so doing encouraged regular competitive elections and the refinement of the electoral machinery to facilitate this governance, all cemented by the international observance of election exercises.

This by-product of the era of structural adjustment is now firmly rooted in a liberal perception of democracy and good governance that has become globalised. However, it strikes at the root of traditional concepts of national sovereignty. Certainly within traditional definitions, subjective issues such as how democracy is defined were to be left up to persons within a nation to decide. The demand that recipient nations conform to western liberal conceptions of democracy therefore violates these traditional understandings of sovereignty. Ironically, the liberal democracy in the US has been shown to be susceptible to influence from the American upper class and by extension the corporate community. This sector of society has been shown to heavily influence the legislative agenda and opinions at both the state and local levels due to the existence of an elaborate committee system and network of lobbyists (Domhoff 1967).

II. INTEGRATION, NATIONAL SOVEREIGNTY AND THE ROLE OF THE NGO

These trends identified above are securely locked in the global system and supported by an international philosophy of neo-liberalism that is spreading exponentially. The small or micro state, such as exists in the Caribbean, is therefore left with little other alternative but to pursue developmental policies as prescribed by the global community. Individual models, such as those evolving in Grenada and Jamaica in the 70s, are unlikely to be successful since the global community is becoming stronger, more intrusive and remains committed to a liberal ideological stance. Initiatives to influence meaningful change within this system have been attempted. The initiative known as the New International Economic Order (NIEO), designed to redistribute the world's wealth more equitably and pursued within the UN framework, failed largely because it ran counter to developed nations' economic objectives. Developing countries therefore need to identify alternatives that attempt to preserve some measure of sovereignty and allow their nationals to determine, to some extent, their own development path.

II. [I] NATIONAL SOVEREIGNTY IN THE CARIBBEAN

Watson[3] has noted that sovereignty should not be treated as a static concept, but constantly needs to be redefined and renegotiated based on the dynamics of the global environment.This has, however, not happened and instead much of the literature relating to the issue of sovereignty has been concerned with the legal or jurisdictional aspects as manifested in the institution known as the state. Certainly the state is the basis on which sovereignty is exercised and this is a reality of international law and a necessary starting point for any analysis of the state. It is on this basis that a state identifies leaders, passes legislation and is recognised by other states as having the legal authority to do so. However, as Watson points out, the dynamics of the global environment require that our concept of sovereignty be reassessed frequently since several variable and external factors can affect the efficacy with which such activities are conducted.

Azcuy (1995) notes that even before independence it is clear that colonies were being perceived by some as states. Recently Barbados' parliament celebrated 350 years in existence, a celebration that was controversial but conveyed a sense that the institution was seen to have had a character of its own and exercising some amount of sovereignty, long before independence and during a time when the largest section of the population was barred from participation in the selection of its members.The fact that this was seen as a legitimate institution at that time, as is the democratic and independent institution that succeeds it today, demonstrates the dynamic nature of sovereignty and state classifications. Similarly the failure of the International Trade Organisation (ITO), largely due to its perceived negative impact on sovereignty, but success of the WTO some five decades later places the sovereignty of the state within the realities of a changing global environment.

Sovereignty therefore has other characteristics which are themselves subject to reinterpretation. As Azcuy (1995, 139) suggests it includes the right to self-determination, a political concept that also includes economic and cultural aspects. However these concepts only have significance when interpreted within a legal definition of a state, or some interstate association that is internationally recognised, allowing for recognition of the national entity as part of an international family of nations.

Watson[4] consolidates several of these characteristics in his reference to 'popular sovereignty.' The insertion of the word popular, however, does more than communicate the inclusion of political and cultural dimensions. It also suggests that in the definition of these there should be a certain amount of consensus regarding what cultural and political components are appropriate at various points in time. Such consensus appears relatively simple when one considers that regular elections are held in most Caribbean countries where the entire adult population chooses between competing political parties, thus allowing people to indicate their support via the ballot. It can, however, be demonstrated that this process has and will convey a less than accurate perspective of popular opinion, a deficiency that creates an opening for alternative methods of ensuring the maintenance of democracy.

Earlier reference to the Domhoff (1967) thesis suggests that a similar pattern of influence might be occurring in the Caribbean countries, since these are similarly organised liberal democracies. Unfortunately no comprehensive studies have ever been conducted on this issue, making it difficult to come to any concrete conclusions. What is certain is that the pattern of gladiatorial politics in the Caribbean involves canvassing large areas, electronic propaganda distribution and satisfying the traditional appetite for social assistance directly from candidates' pockets. These activities require funding that would likely come from corporate or individual donors who presumably would exercise some amount of influence over the legislative programme of an elected government. While the abilities of a particular candidate cannot be totally discounted from the process, the ability to effectively reach substantial sections of the population and win their support often depends on the level of funding available to a particular candidate.

In as much as several Caribbean countries are involved in IMF/World Bank structural adjustment programmes and because of the pervasiveness of the global governance network, several Caribbean populations might find little difference between political parties' programmes and ideologies. This is a fairly recent phenomena in Caribbean countries such as Jamaica where the socialist policies of the Peoples National Party (PNP) were diametrically opposed to the more liberal JLP stance during the 70's and early 80's. It is not, however, unfamiliar in Barbados where both major political parties have historically had a mixed agenda of socialist and liberal programmes. In an article entitled 'Shake Your Manifesto: see if what falls out is any different from the others' (Sunday Express, November 5, 1995), Kim Johnson commented extensively on the similarity of manifestos in the 1995 Trinidad and Tobago election, a coincidence that has become commonplace in the Caribbean. The ideological path therefore seems fairly well established and one's choice of a particular party could not possibly reflect an ideological preference. Instead, a party preference could be predicated on a traditional basis, or in respect of a specific programme that the individual prefers. The point on the traditional basis for party support is easily demonstrated by reference to the fact that in the Caribbean countries of Jamaica, Barbados and Trinidad and Tobago, major political parties have usually received no less than 20 per cent[5] of the popular vote in each election (Emmanuel 1992).

Closely related to the similarity in the ideological position of the major political parties in the Caribbean, is the demonstrated disinterest in the political process as manifested in electoral participation. In Barbados, Jamaica and Trinidad and Tobago voter turnout exceeded 80 per cent[6] shortly after independence and while in no case has there been a steady decline, recent elections have all reflected a lower voter turnout. In Barbados the 1991 electoral turnout was 63 per cent with the 1994 figures being even lower. Similarly Trinidad and Tobago had a 63 per cent turnout in 1991 and Jamaica a 78 per cent turnout in 1989, with the data showing similar declines throughout the Leeward and Windward islands.

Elections therefore cannot be said to give a clear indication of popular opinion since in some cases close to 40 per cent, or more than one third of the voting population, does not express an opinion. Moreover, where this opinion is expressed, it appears to be motivated more by historical loyalty to a political party than by a preference for any party's philosophy or programme. In countries where there is a large rural population such as Guyana and Suriname or, alternatively where illiteracy rates are higher, this situation would be exacerbated leading to greater under-representation of the population.

The importance of elections stems from the fact that they are the single event that forms the basis of our liberal democratic system, a system that interprets the Greek words *demos* and *kratia* (rule by the people) to be representative in nature (Bogdanor 1992, 166).These events have been heavily relied upon to gauge public opinion on all matters, including the society's perception of what sovereignty is interpreted to mean at any point in time. Since this basis today appears objectionable, the question arises of how do we determine public opinion or 'popular opinion' regarding what constitutes sovereignty and how would a people express their right to self-determination. The NGO can play a significant role in this regard, an issue that will be fully ventilated below. However, the apparent conflictual relationship between integration and sovereignty must first be addressed.

II. [II] INTEGRATION AND SOVEREIGNTY

Since sovereignty is often given a legal and geographical interpretation, there appears to be a conflict that would arise where countries associated with each other in such a way that the power to make certain decisions was surrendered to a regional body.This contradiction has been the root cause of much vacillation within CARICOM regarding the non-implementation of decisions and failure to forge closer unity. The superimposition of regional structures violates the historical relationship that has existed in the Caribbean between the representative and his constituents, especially in small societies where such relationships are often personal. Furthermore where the regional organisation makes decisions in the interest of the community that run counter to the interest of small sectors of it, the temptation is always to seek redress at the national level, where the representative can be pressured by the electoral process. In instances where there is no elected regional body to form an alternative relationship at that level, the situation is further complicated.

The CARICOM treaty calls for the 'establishment of a common market regime; ...the coordination of foreign policies of Member States; ... and functional cooperation' (Treaty of Chaguaramas, Article 4). Arguably cooperation in these areas is necessary to secure the development of the region. However, activity in these areas is equally symbolic of the retention of national sovereignty. Control of foreign affairs is a major power that was withheld from colonies even under the most liberal of colonial arrangements and it is not surprising that ex-colonies jealously guard this power and are hesitant to follow the dictates of the CARICOM Standing Committee on Foreign Affairs. Similarly activities relating to the common market include currency issues and other symbols of national sovereignty and are frustrated by past experiences that have shown how economies could be adversely affected where joint action is pursued[7].

The earlier discussion on globalisation has demonstrated that in none of these areas identified for joint action can Caribbean countries really exercise any genuine choice characteristic of self-determination. This is not a feature of the absence of the legal mechanism to do so, but a reality of the global environment in which we operate. Trade agendas are set for the region by the protocols of GATT, WTO and indeed by several other conventions such as Lomé, that give small nations little room to manoeuvre. Monetary matters are similarly regulated by the uselessness of local currencies and the volatility of hard currencies on the international market. In this regard the symbolic nature of a national currency is just that and has little real value. If we look to the other areas of foreign affairs and functional cooperation, these have to be viewed against the background of an international power, whose influence is easily demonstrated by reference to the Helms-Burton Act. The issues that the region's countries need to make an impact on, such as tourism, the environment and drug interdiction, are all incapable of being dealt with at the national level.

The challenge that integration therefore answers is that it provides a larger geopolitical space where small countries working together could possibly achieve that which they are unable to achieve locally. Such achievements could be in the form of effective action such as the change in CARICOM's foreign policy stance towards Cuba, but would most likely come in the form of the region's ability to influence the global agenda to some extent. Such was the thinking behind the Independent West Indian Commission's (WIC's) proposal that CARICOM 'by treaty agree to the pooling of certain of their sovereignties and to [the] exercising [of] them collectively in certain respects' (WIC 1992, 466), a phrase that characterises how integration facilitates genuine sovereignty.

By extension the achievement of 'popular sovereignty' in the Caribbean would be to some extent derived from the location of general economic, cultural and political themes with which the region's people can identify and seek to actualise as part of their developmental objectives. The dimensions of the regional vehicle would simply be designed to ensure that self-determination could be achieved within the constraints of the present global environment. To be sure, such a community would be diverse since Caribbean popular culture represents a potpourri of 'the cultural legacies of Africa, Europe, Asia and Indigenous America.'[8] Hence attention needs to be paid to the unifying characteristics of language, history and common legal and administrative systems, instead of the divisive cultural peculiarities that are present in any single nation state (Demas 1995, 65). The task of identifying the geographical space within which popular sovereignty can be exercised and the components thereof is a task for which the NGO is ideally suited, since it embodies an extension of the concept of representative democracy by empowering several sectors of the Caribbean societies.

II. [III] THE NGO, INTEGRATION AND NATIONAL SOVEREIGNTY IN THE CARIBBEAN

The term NGO embraces a wide cross section of organisations that are not established for profit making purposes. Because of the wide variety of NGOs, Korten (1990, 2) offers the following categories for purposes of consolidation:

In the Caribbean as in several developing societies, people have put their faith and resources in the hands of government in the hope that sustainable development will be delivered to them. Therefore, the failure of development models of the post-independence period has called into question both the capacity of governments and the nature of development itself. As a result there has emerged a role for civil society in defining development and we have witnessed a rediscovery of private sector involvement and a new role being identified for NGOs in development. These organisations are, according to Nettleford[9], ideally suited to work in collusion with the private sector and government in the determination of values 'commonly regarded as supportive of civil society.' They can be said to embody the people's power essential to the functioning of the society that is complemented by the economic power of the private sector and the political power of the government (Korten 1990, 96).

Governments in the Caribbean have a history of involving NGOs in the business of government because of the close association of the leading political parties with the trade union movement. There has not, however, been any systematic attempt to involve other NGOs in the process of defining issues and creating policy. More recently the Jamaican government has actually established mechanisms for collaboration between itself and the NGO movement and the Barbados government has articulated a position supporting similar involvement although the 'social partners'[10] approach of the former Barbados government reflected a narrow definition of the concept.

Archer (1992) has noted that increasingly international non-governmental organisations (INGOs) have become important actors in international relations, because of their interaction with national governments and their relations among themselves. Ghils (1992) counted some 23,000 organisations that were registered with either international or national agencies and estimated a larger multiple of this number to actually be in existence.These are especially useful in specialised agencies where 'consultative status' is accorded to these INGOs in order to benefit from their contribution to policy development. Regional organisations such as the EU and CARICOM, CARIFORUM and the Association of Caribbean States (ACS) have legitimised INGOs by conferring either 'observer' or 'consultative status,' that has paralleled the local situation. This status has facilitated the creation of specialised sub-groups that address particular issues and have direct influence on multilateral institutions and agreements.

The Convention establishing the ACS implicitly provides for the participation of NGOs in the association's work by empowering the Ministerial Council to 'determine the Social Partners which it recognises and accepts and define their roles' (ACS 1994), a definition that has since specifically provided for NGOs to be accepted as social partners so long as they 'contributed to the programs, plans and objectives established by the Convention' (ACS 1995, 5/95). Participation in the ACS Ministerial Council meetings is consultative, facilitating the right to speak without the right to vote and is presumably designed to facilitate the contribution of specialised knowledge where the Council deems necessary.To date the CPDC has regularly been invited to attend and participate in meetings of the ACS.

Similar recognition can be identified in the EU where a Caribbean reference group with substantial NGO input has been mandated to propose a successor to the Lomé agreement.At the UN level, the NGO has been playing a significant role in the definition of issues as has been evidenced in their contribution to the 1992 Earth Summit, where an adjunct Global Forum for NGOs was simultaneously convened and the Global Conference on the Sustainable Development of Small Island Developing States where a similar forum was established.

Comparable legitimacy has been accorded by the MFIs as evidenced in the establishment of a World Bank-NGO committee providing a formal coordinating focal point for the Bank's dealings with NGOs. Here activity takes place in four main areas:

- operational collaboration, in projects and programmes;
- development education;
- policy dialogue between the World Bank and NGOs, particularly on poverty alleviation and environmental issues; and
- public frameworks for NGOs (Cernea 1988, 29).

Because of the highly influential position of the World Bank identified above, such NGO interaction allows the NGOs to influence the development agenda of countries in the most effective way.

French (1995) has linked the NGO to the process of integration by identifying it as a developmental tool which the NGO can assist in shaping, since developmental efforts have all too often been externally defined. The involvement of the NGO allows people to participate directly in the process of setting our agenda for development. In this regard NGO involvement in the integration movement would seek to ensure a people-centred approach, ensuring that integration seeks to address more than esoteric issues. It helps to ensure that integration remains a developmental tool that is securely focused on addressing the needs of Caribbean people.

NGOs often act on behalf of severely marginalised groups such as small farmers, women, the unemployed and young people who are unable to influence government's macroeconomic policies but are nevertheless, or as a result, most severely affected by such policies. In the areas of structural adjustment, the Caribbean NGO movement has become a fierce advocate on behalf of these disenfranchised groups. They have as a result compiled a substantial body of information on these sectors and, moreover, perfected methods of popular communication that can prove invaluable to the process of democratisation.

The NGO movement has consistently articulated its position on both general and specific development issues in the Caribbean. These positions were consolidated into a perspective on sustainable human development prior to the UN Conference on Small Island Developing States. The principles articulated by the NGO coalition around which human development in the Caribbean should be pursued are worth repeating:

- EQUITY between genders, generations, racial and ethnic groups, rural and urban populations, disabled and specially challenged people, rich and poor, countries of the industrialised North and those of the dependent South;

- PARTICIPATION in decision making at all levels, as well as in the implementation of policies and programmes;
- WHOLISM ensuring that social, cultural, economic, ecological and political considerations are taken into account;
- SUSTAINABILITY of all aspects of development; and
- SELF-RELIANCE[11].

The NGO in the Caribbean offers a bonus to the regional integration movement that has been of substantial assistance in accelerating it and comes as a result of the fact that Caribbean NGOs are either regional in character, or alternatively articulate within a network of regional organisations. NGO activity has therefore been of tremendous assistance in bringing people in the region face to face and as a result has encouraged social integration. Often local organisations have sought regional action on local issues and found through their association with like-minded organisations in the region that the issues affecting them are similar and better solved at a regional level. Such has been the experience in the grass roots sectors of the Caribbean where organisations like the Windward Islands Farmers' Association (WINFA) have brought together people who would otherwise not have come into contact with each other and united them around common issues that impact on them. Regionalism is therefore inadvertently marketed to these grassroots people as a solution to some of their more pertinent problems. Historically, Anglophone Caribbean integration has not appealed to these sectors of society resulting in episodes like the Jamaica referendum of 1961 that called for a withdrawal from the West Indies Federation. However, NGOs have succeeded in locating popular support for Caribbean integration in their ability to address issues affecting some of the most disenfranchised people in the Caribbean.

The earlier reference to NGO methods of popular communication is also relevant here, since with many grassroots organisations remoteness alienates them from national policy making, and even more from regional issues. The existence of networks that facilitate communication with these sectors can be used to promote and create support for Caribbean integration that is being pursued by governments and removes the potential friction in the long term. The NGOs therefore, fill several voids regarding Caribbean integration in that they give meaningful definition to the concept of popular opinion, the basis of popular sovereignty and moreover assist in the garnering of support to grassroots sectors of the Caribbean through their advanced communication network.

II. [IV] SHORTCOMINGS OF NGO-AUGMENTED GOVERNANCE

While not detracting from the tremendous potential of the NGO movement, it should be noted that involvement of NGOs in the process of government is not without problems and it is important to discuss these during this period of NGO organisational growth in order that these might be overcome. Cernea (1988, 18-19) relates the shortcomings of local NGOs to their sise, limited technical capacity and short shelf life. He asserts that by their very voluntary nature, several limitations are inherent since an organisational structure is difficult to develop on that basis. The technical capacity of NGOs in these local situations is limited by an expected absence of staff and research facilities. As a result the activities pursued might be deliberately narrowed and restricted to a time frame where skills are available. These organisations will not have the opportunity to gain national respect and as a result will develop a very limited and narrow focus and be transitory in nature.

One of the results of a high level of specialisation in NGOs and the resulting narrow focus is the multiplicity of them arising to facilitate a reaction to almost every single issue on the developmental agenda. While the number of NGO networks registered with the CPDC in 1995 was only 21, this merely represents the number of regional sub-regional or national agencies with a regional perspective. The actual number of NGOs is far greater. The multiplicity of NGOs is not a problem in itself. Indeed, a large NGO sector strengthens the democratic fabric of a nation. However where the number of NGOs spirals it poses problems as governmental agencies attempt to identify the appropriate organisations with which an alliance should be formed. The existence of a regional umbrella agency (CPDC) has assisted considerably in providing some structure for the potentially large number of organisations in existence but this does not prevent new organisations, or even umbrella agencies from emerging and seeking legitimacy. The question then arises as to which organisation warrants recognition, a decision that could have severe political consequences either way.

The converse situation is also possible where the unregulated NGO environment could result in under-representation in several areas, as there is over-representation in others. The plight of women in the Caribbean has generated substantial interest and justified concern. Consequently there has been an over-representation of NGOs concerned with women's issues. Similarly the family has generated substantial interest along with matters relating to the poor. These are all noble and important issues, but the bias here reflects a potential problem with NGOs that could be self-defeating.

Fowler (1991, 69) distinguishes NGOs from governments and commercial enterprises since the latter two derive their resources from those who they serve, while NGOs do not. As a result NGOs are often beholding to donors of official aid and can easily be encouraged to shift their accountability from their original constituents. This is especially so where the organisation becomes large and bureaucratic, having to support a cadre of employees with long term contracts and commitments. With the best of devotion to a philosophical position, a cash-strapped organisation might succumb to the temptation to alter a position slightly to facilitate the demands of donors. The current interest being shown in NGOs by the World Bank and the attempts to inculcate them into its formal structure raises the potential for influence that is similar to the IMF/World Bank conditionality problem identified above. To date, no comprehensive study of the influence that funding agencies have on NGOs has been conducted in the Caribbean hence one can go no further than to say that the potential exists for influence. NGOs must become professional and raise funds, but in so doing will need to strengthen their philosophical position, since funding is the easiest way to achieve influence and undue influence at this level could easily nullify the utility of such organisations.

III. CARIBBEAN INTEGRATION - CARICOM VERSUS ACS

The WIC called for the establishment of the ACS, which has created some confusion as to what should be the appropriate regional organisation to secure Caribbean integration. The logic behind such an association lies in the fact that CARICOM, as it is now constituted, comprises only 5.7 million people which does not provide the optimum sise for the development of economies of scale in our global economy. As a result we needed to identify larger markets that would allow us to realise such economies. The countries of the Caribbean archipelago that were not members of CARICOM along with other mainland countries with a littoral on the Caribbean sea therefore appeared to be the logical countries with which CARICOM should attempt to form an association. Such an association produced a regional grouping of just over 200 million people with a GDP that would allow it to make some small impact on the global community, or alternatively guard against total domination by larger economic blocs such as NAFTA and the EU. The choice of appropriate countries is presumably predicated on the belief that our geographical proximity, shared history of exploitation and similarity of people are cumulatively enough for our people to achieve a consensus on development issues that promote the development of all countries.

It is clear, however, that a consensus would be that much harder to achieve within this wider community since, notwithstanding the similarities, many differences would be exacerbated within this diverse community. The fact that CARICOM accounts for only three per cent of the population of the community is significant especially since many of the ACS countries such as Columbia and Venezuela have relatively well-developed economies. CARICOM will therefore find itself in a similar position to the LDCs within CARICOM, that need to seek concessions in order that the playing field might eventually be levelled.

At the same time that the ACS is being developed, CARICOM is attempting to further deepen the association amongst its members by completing the establishment of a Common Market that necessitates an even greater surrender of sovereignty. Already steps have been taken towards the achievement of freedom of movement within CARICOM and the phasing in of the Common External Tariff (CET) is almost complete. In addition, discussion of monetary union, or at least the reintroduction of the CMCF, is currently taking place suggesting that CARICOM is approaching a quasi-political union that appears to run counter to the loose association that the ACS represents.

CARICOM within the ACS is comparable to the OECS within CARICOM, an analogy that eliminates possible confusion caused by this apparent plurality. The organisations have similar objectives and as a result can easily coexist. Indeed since the level of homogeneity within CARICOM is greater, it can act to establish a suitable platform with which ACS articulation can take place. Problems such as the expected trade imbalance between the larger and smaller countries in the ACS can be considerably minimised by the existence of a strong CARICOM group. Hence the processes of deepening and widening should take place simultaneously since the institutions are likely to compliment each other. In this regard NGOs will need to be involved at both levels to ensure that a focus is maintained at both levels and that the necessary networks are strengthened among ACS communities, a necessity that suggests the need for a Pan-Caribbean NGO umbrella body.

IV. NGOS IN THE PAST AND FUTURE OF CARIBBEAN INTEGRATION

The role that this paper anticipates for NGOs in the region will ultimately require some change in the way the Caribbean's leaders perceive governance at a regional level. Such a re-orientation is necessary if the region is to benefit fully from the enhanced democracy that NGOs bring to regionalism. The nature of and solutions to problems in the global economy today require a far more broad-based approach than can be provided by the bases upon which historical structures for regional organisations were established.

IV. [I] HISTORICAL ROLE OF NGOS IN THE PROCESS OF INTEGRATION

Attempts at Caribbean integration can be traced back to the earliest settlement of the English-speaking Caribbean countries where various methods were attempted to jointly administer the islands. The nature of the demand for integration during this period was largely one of reducing administrative cost to the metropole, hence there was little scope for the involvement of any interest group, outside of the more wealthy settlers. Greater self-government and independence, however, provided opportunities for the involvement of several interests in the movement towards Caribbean integration. This opportunity was seised mainly by the Caribbean labour movement that later became the political directorate that used Caribbean unity as the vehicle to carry the colonies toward independence. Throughout this era, the labour interest was the only discernible NGO making a significant contribution to the integration movement.

With the collapse of the West Indies Federation in 1962, the region moved toward the establishment of the Caribbean Free Trade Area (CARIFTA). The fact that CARIFTA was framed around private sector trade, afforded the involvement of more genuinely non-governmental interests in the movement toward Caribbean unity. CARIFTA gave birth to CARICOM, an association that called for the 'coordination of the foreign policies of Member States; and functional cooperation' (Treaty of Chaguaramas Art. 4), in addition to the establishment of a common market building on the CARIFTA idea. The inclusion of functional cooperation in the CARICOM treaty was refined to encourage 'the promotion of greater understanding among its peoples and the advancement of their social, cultural and technological development.' This objective has presented an avenue that could genuinely accommodate the involvement of NGOs.

In reality, the foregoing has provided little genuine opportunity for NGOs to play a significant role, because the substantive thrust of Anglophone Caribbean integration is centred around the CARICOM Secretariat, the activities it organises and the standing committee structure that does not easily accommodate diverse interest groups. Since matters pertaining to trade and the common market dominate the Secretariat, NGOs that speak to wider issues of development have found little comfort within the annals of CARICOM. The need to further integrate NGOs and indeed all social partners into the work of CARICOM was alluded to in the CARICOM Charter of Civil Society (WIC 1992, 492) that has led to a CARICOM decision to comprehensively study the NGO movement, but the actual outcome of this interest is yet to be realised.

While CARICOM is still very much a functioning entity, it has been complemented by the more comprehensive ACS which is seen to be taking centre-stage in regional matters as increasingly CARICOM is becoming marginalised. The ACS has indicated by way of its association with the CPDC that it is interested in involving NGOs in its work, a development that will allow for substantial influence. In reality, however, the inability to vote, the initial focus of the ACS on trade, tourism and transport (ACS 1995) and the association's relative looseness weakens the scope for deeper NGO involvement.

V. [II] STRUCTURES FOR NGO PARTICIPATION IN CARIBBEAN UNITY

The governance of an organisation heavily influences its role, functions, financing and impact. Hence, a renewed approach to governance of regional institutions is central to an improved role for NGOs. Currently, policy within CARICOM and the ACS is directed by the Conference of Heads of Government of CARICOM and the Meeting of Heads of State of the ACS. As the names suggest, these bodies comprise the heads of all countries who are members of the organisation, a bias that inadvertently excludes a large section of the population of the region and, more importantly, several interests. Hence, an 'ideal' governance body for these organisations would embrace leaders from select NGO umbrellas within the region, holding status equivalent to that of the national leaders. In so doing, a governance partnership would be created at the apex of these organisations. While it is appreciated that the various governments would need to create the necessary facility to allow for this representation, mechanisms would need to be designed to ensure that the maximum independence of these representatives is facilitated. Once this central governance partnership is in place, it would allow for a modified approach to several issues such as the scope of operation, activities to be pursued and funding arrangements.

The above arrangement does not represent a radical departure from what currently obtains within regional organisations throughout the world, since it was already highlighted that most of these have voluntarily involved NGOs in their discussions and defined roles for them in the organisations. However within regional and international organisations currently, NGOs can, at best, expect observer status as has happened within CARICOM, the ACS and the EU, since they are essentially governmental organisations. The appropriateness of this structure to developed countries cannot be challenged. Indeed this arrangement has been the basis of the successful EU. It is, however, being argued that LDCs in the Caribbean have different demands. The Caribbean countries are characteristic of LDCs in that they are diverse communities requiring a rapid policy reaction to various problems. The inclusion of NGOs in a structure of governance, therefore, allows for several diverse interests and talents to be co-opted in the design of appropriate policies to be pursued by the community, in addition to guaranteeing widespread support for policy initiatives.

This alternative approach raises several questions. Significant among these is the mechanism for determining participation in such a governance partnership, along with legitimacy issues and the financial implications to the regional organisation. These and related issues would need to be addressed, but do not detract from the tremendous potential offered by this approach to governance of regional organisations. It would, however, create an opportunity for NGOs in the region to play a significant role in the integration process and furthermore ensures that regional organisations adequately address issues of concern to all sectors of the Caribbean's population. Integration, therefore, would genuinely become a means to an end of development in a rapidly changing environment. Such development requires a wide definition of its parameters and an orientation that identifies integration as a means to an end of development, a goal that would hopefully be achieved by this approach.

CONCLUSION

The major reality of globalisation is the increasing irrelevance of the state, alongside even greater increases in the pervasiveness of international governance and multilateral agencies. This reality is exacerbated in developing countries due to their peripheral status in the world community and is manifested in several specific ways. The foregoing has demonstrated ways in which these impacts on the sovereignty of Caribbean people have been perpetuated and how the potential for self-fulfilment has been removed. Actual manifestations of this erosion of sovereignty have resulted in the Caribbean being exploited in the furtherance of the objectives of developed countries and transnational corporations, generating debt burdens, poverty and substantial alienation. The Caribbean appears to be locked securely into a global political economy that leaves few alternatives to the neo-liberal ideology with all its attendant hardships.

Regionalism, or the development of economic communities and trade blocs, appears to offer a platform for developing countries to increase their bargaining power in the global community, hence facilitating greater independence of the grouping. The group therefore expressly agrees to exercise its power jointly, in the hope that it can thereby be more genuinely exercised. Such has been the experience of the EU and, while the Caribbean is not anticipating anything of that magnitude, a Caribbean association could substantially increase our international presence and ability to influence the global agenda. Caribbean integration can therefore become an effective developmental tool for the region.

NGOs have been gaining legitimacy both locally and internationally because of their outstanding contribution to the definition of the development process and, importantly, their ability to enfranchise previously disenfranchised sectors of the Caribbean societies. Cumulatively they have come to represent a popular culture in the Caribbean that is indispensable to the integration movement and have furthermore developed a regional network of their own that greatly facilitates integration. Organisationally, these groups have been considerably professionalised and improved upon in their organisational structures and as a result have become indispensable to Caribbean integration and Caribbean development generally, locating it within a people oriented development framework.

In order that the full potential of NGOs be realised, it is necessary that they be empowered in integrative organisations. This will require some concessions on the part of governments in the region, allowing NGO representatives to share in the governance of regional organisations. Some progress has already been made in that regard, but while participatory status partially addresses the issue, a further step is needed to ensure that NGOs can make a direct link between the popular opinions that they represent and the action taken by regional institutions. Such a modification would set Caribbean regional institutions apart from their international counterparts, but is necessary to ensure that in the Caribbean there is the fullest possible participation in the process of development.

NOTES

1. Thompson (1992) adopts a less pessimistic view of international market regulation, suggesting that while controls exist, the activities being controlled are identified in a haphazard manner.
2. Sub-Saharan Africa: From Crisis to Sustainable Growth: A Long-Term Perspective Study, Washington: World Bank, 1989.
3. Professor H. Watson made these comments during the course of a Seminar entitled 'Integration and National Sovereignty in the Caribbean,' USB, Caracas, June 20-22, 1996.
4. Ibid.
5. The reference to 20 per cent is a generalisation that appreciates that in Jamaica close to 30 per cent of the votes are split between the two parties and in Trinidad and Tobago the PNM has traditionally received in the vicinity of 40 per cent of the popular support at the polls.
6. Data taken from Emmanuel 1992, 8-17.
7. Reference is made here to the failed CARICOM Multilateral Clearing Facility (CMCF).
8. Extract from a statement by Prime Minister Owen Arthur of Barbados to the Miami Summit, December 1994.
9. Preface to Challenges in Caribbean Development: Interventions of Non-Governmental Organisations at the CARICOM Regional Economic Conference, February 1991.
10. The former DLP administration established a consultative council comprising representatives of the trade unions, staff associations and private sector.
11. NGO position adopted at the Regional Meeting of Caribbean NGOs in Preparation for SIDS, July 9-11, 1993, Trinidad, p.1.

REFERENCES

ARTICLES, BOOKS AND OTHER PUBLISHED MATERIAL:

Archer, Clive. International Organisations. New York: Routledge, 1992.

Azcuy, Hugo. 'The New World Order, National Sovereignty and Self-determination in the Caribbean.' In Globalisation, Integration and Human Rights in the Caribbean. Documents Series, no. 11. Bogotá: Instituto Latinoamericano de Servicios Alternativos, 1995.

Bogdanor, Vernon. (ed.) 1987 Reprint The Blackwell Encyclopedia of Political Science. Massachusetts: Blackwell, 1992.

Brown, Seyom. New Forces, Old Forces and the Future of World Politics. Glenview, Illinois: Scott Foresman and Company, 1988.

New Forces, Old Forces, and the Future of World Politics. Post-Cold War edition. New York: Harper Collins, 1995.

Campanella, Miriam L. 'The Effects of Globalisation and Turbulence on the Policy-Making Process.' Government and Opposition 28, no. 2 (Spring 1993): 190-205.

Cernea, Michael M. Non-Governmental Organisations and Local Development. World Bank Discussion Papers No. 40. Washington: World Bank, 1988.

Daily Express (Trinidad and Tobago) February 27, 1997.

Demas, William G. West Indian Development and the Deepening and Widening of the Caribbean Community. Kingston: Institute of Social and Economic Research, University of the West Indies, 1995.

Domhoff, William G. Who Rules America? Englewood Cliffs; New Jersey: Prentice Hall, 1967.

Duncan, Neville. 'Globalisation or Recolonisation: Forcing the Integration Imperative.' In Caribbean Integration: The OECS Experience Revisited, edited by Neville Duncan. Kingston: Friedrich Ebert Siftung, 1995.

Mechanisms of Impoverishment in the Anglophone Caribbean: the role of the Bretton Woods institutions and the recommendations of Caribbean NGOs. St. Michael: Caribbean Policy Development Centre, 1995.

Emmanuel, Patrick. Elections and Party Systems in the Commonwealth Caribbean. St. Michael: Caribbean Development Research Services, 1992.

Evans, T., Carlos Castro and Jennifer Jones. Structural Adjustment and the Public Sector in Central America and the Caribbean. Managua: CRIES, 1995.

Ferguson, Tyrone. Structural Adjustment and Good Governance. Georgetown: Public Affairs Consulting Enterprise, 1995.

Fowler, Alan. 'The Role of NGOs in Changing State-Society Relations: Perspectives from Eastern and Southern Africa.' Development Policy Review Vol. 9, 1991.

French, Joan. 'Non-Governmental Organisations and Regional Integration'. In Caribbean Integration: The OECS Experience Revisited, edited by Neville Duncan. Kingston: Friedrich Ebert Stiftung, 1995.

'Role of Public, Private and NGO Sectors:The Role of Public and Private Sector Organisations and NGOs in Development.' In Challenges in Caribbean Development: Interventions of Non-Governmental Organisations at The CARICOM Regional Economic Conference, compiled by Joan French. Bridgetown: Caribbean Policy Development Centre, 1992.

Ghils, Paul. 'International Civil Society: International Non-Governmental Organisations in the International System,' International Social Science Journal. Vol. 44, No. 3, (August) 1993.

Gilpin, Robert. 'The Politics of Transnational Economic Relations.' In Transnational Relations and World Politics, edited by Robert O. Keohane and Joseph S. Nye, Jr. Cambridge, Massachusetts: Harvard University Press, 1970.

Girvan, Norman. 'Jamaica Stagnation and Indebtedness 1973-1989'. In The Debt Problem of Small Peripheral Economies: Case Studies from the Caribbean and Central America, edited by Norman Girvan et al. Kingston: Association of Caribbean Economists, 1990.

Held, David, and Anthony McGrew. 'Globalisation and the Liberal Democratic State.' Government and Opposition 28, no. 2 (Spring 1993): 261-288.

Hosten-Craig, Jennifer. The Effect of the North American Free Trade Agreement on the Commonwealth Caribbean. NY: Edwin Mellen Press, 1992.

Independent West Indian Commission. Time For Action; The Report of the West Indian Commission. Black Rock; Barbados: The Independent West Indian Commission, 1989.

Ionescu, Ghita. 'The Impact of the Information Revolution on Parliamentary Sovereignties.' Government and Opposition 28, no. 2 (Spring 1993): 221-241.

Kirton, Alan. 'Regional Cooperation: A Single Community for all Caribbean People.' In Challenges in Caribbean Development: Interventions of Non-Governmental Organisations at the CARICOM Regional Economic Conference, compiled by Joan French. Bridgetown: Caribbean Policy Development Centre, 1992.

Korten, David. Getting to the 21st Century: Voluntary Action and the Global Agenda. West Hartford; Connecticut: Kumarian, 1990.

LeFranc, Elsie. (ed) Consequences of Structural Adjustment: A Review of the Jamaican Experience. Kingston: Canoe Press, 1994.

Levitt, Kari P. The Origins and Consequences of Jamaica's Debt Crisis 1970-1990. Kingston: Consortium Graduate School of Social Sciences, 1991.

McAfee, Kathy. Storm Signals: Structural Adjustment and Development Alternatives in the Caribbean. London: Zed Books, 1991.

Parry, Geraint. 'The Interweaving of Foreign and Domestic Policy Making.' Government and Opposition 28, no. 2 (Spring 1993): 143-151.

Payne, Anthony. 'Liberal Economics versus Electoral Politics in Jamaica' in Anthony Payne and Paul Sutton. Modern Caribbean Politics. Kingston: Ian Randle, 1993.

Raghavan, Chakravarthi. 'Uruguay Round: the Amrit or the Poisoned Chalice?', Third World Economics, June 1-15, 1993.

Robinson, Mark. 'Will Political Conditionality Work?' IDS Bulletin, Vol. 24, No. 1, January 1993.

Rojas, Onofre. 'The New World Order, Nation-state, Sovereignty and Self-determination in the Caribbean.' In Globalisation, Integration and Human Rights in the Caribbean. Documents Series, no. 11. Bogotá: Instituto Latinoamericano de Servicios Alternativos, 1995.

Saxe-Fernández, John. 'Globalisation: Geoeconomic and Geopolitical Aspects' In Globalisation, Integration and Human Rights in the Caribbean. Documents Series, no. 11. Bogotá: Instituto Latinoamericano de Servicios Alternativos, 1995.

Stevens, C. 'The Caribbean and Europe 1992: Endgame?' Development Policy Review 9, no. 3 (September 1991): 265-283.

Strange, Susan. Casino Capitalism. Cambridge, Massachusetts: Blackwell, 1986.

States and Markets. London: Printer, 1988.

Sunday Express (Trinidad and Tobago) November 5, 1995, March 02, 1997.

Thompson, Janice. 'Explaining the Regulation of Transnational Practices: A State Building Approach.' In Governance Without Government: Order and Change in World Politics, edited by James N. Rosenau and Ernst-Otto Czempiel. Cambridge: Cambridge University Press, 1992.

Underhill, Geoffrey R. D. 'Conceptualizing the Changing Global Order'. In Political Economy and the Changing Global Order, edited by Richard Stubbs and Geoffrey R. D. Underhill. London: Macmillan, 1993.

Watson, Hilbourne. (ed.) The Caribbean in the Global Political Economy. Kingston: Ian Randle, 1994.

'Liberalism, the Market, and Globalisation: Issues Affecting Economic and Social Rights in the Caribbean.' In Globalisation, Integration and Human Rights in the Caribbean. Documents Series, no. 11. Bogotá: Instituto Latinoamericano de Servicios Alternativos, 1995.

Wedderburn, Judith. 'The New Sociopolitical Agenda for the Integration Process in the Greater Caribbean.' Paper presented at the SELA International Conference on, Organisations and Social Actors in the Regionalisation Process. Caracas, February 12-13, 1996.

Wickham, Peter W. 'More Shadow than Substance.' Caribbean Affairs. Vol. 7 No. 3 (July/August) 1994.

World Bank. Governance and Development. Washington: World Bank, 1992.

World Development Report 1992. New York: Oxford University Press, 1992.

MISCELLANEOUS DOCUMENTATION:

Association of Caribbean States. Convention Establishing the Association of Caribbean States. Cartagena, 1994.

Inaugural Summit of the Association of Caribbean States. Declaration of Principles and Plan of Action on Tourism, Trade and Transportation. Port of Spain, 1995.

First Ordinary Meeting of the Ministerial Council. Official Records, Agreement no. 4/95. Adoption of the Terms and Conditions for the Participation of Observers in the Meetings of the Ministerial Council and of the Special Committees of the Association of Caribbean States. Guatemala, 1995.

First Ordinary Meeting of the Ministerial Council. Official Records, Agreement no. 5/95. Adoption of the Terms and Conditions for the Participation of Social Partners in the Meetings of the Ministerial Council and the Special Committees of the Association of Caribbean States. Guatemala, 1995.

Caribbean Community. (CARICOM) Treaty Establishing the Caribbean Community (CARICOM). Chaguaramas, 1973.

CPDC Public Forum on GATT, Solidarity House, Barbados, October 1994

Anglophone Caribbean non-state sectors in national integration: a vital step in CARICOM and Greater Caribbean integration

Dr. Neville Duncan is Senior Lecturer in Government and Politics at the University of the West Indies, Cave Hill. He is a member of the Association of Caribbean Economists (ACE) and serves as a consultant to regional NGOs, including the Caribbean Conference of Churches (CCC).

Introduction

This article draws on concrete work of various types of non-state or sub-state organisations to indicate some of their experiences in people-centred governance. It is a critical analysis of the lessons learned from some indicative experiences outlined. The framework utilised suggests different types of non-governmental organisations and therefore some special lessons are identified. The effect of this is to convey the complexity and variability of NGOs as well as their potential to contribute to a system of good governance nationally, and in the anglophone and greater Caribbean.

To be sure, there are other types of non-state actors and the key ones (business and labour) have, in various ways, been involved with the state in tripartite arrangements and social partnerships. Special attention is paid to NGOs other than these in order to argue for their incorporation not merely into the existing scheme of things but to contribute to a new structure of governance. The purpose of this examination is to begin the process of linking central government, local government and a wider set of non-state actors in a relationship which conduces to good governance as the preeminent basis for regional integration.

Most social actors are engaged in regionalisation as a secondary project. The first project is how to create representative umbrella organisations dedicated to research, advocacy and negotiation with a professional core staff. As it stands, governments find it easier to dismiss civil society representatives or selectively choose persons from member organisations because the range, representativeness, consensus and cohesion are inadequate or nonexistent. To become truly relevant for the regionalisation and integration process cohesive, comprehensive and dedicated organisational structure is imperative.

The argument of this piece is that for non-state actors to have a meaningful and continuing role to play in the regionalisation and integration process at the CARICOM and greater Caribbean levels, they must first be in a legitimate and sustainable relationship with their state nationally. There is a growing body of evidence which suggests that in many ways the governments of the CARICOM states have begun to take some steps which conduce to the emergence of a new system of governance. This is manifested in tripartite negotiations (if not agreements) between government, business and labour on a social compact in relation to incomes and prices and hence economic development. Studies have indicated numerous types of arrangements between the state and NGOs/CBOs, domestically, regionally and internationally. Public sector reform has been officially embraced at the CARICOM level and many governments have begun the process in large and smaller ways. Predisposing conditions such as a significant pool of educated and skilled citizens clamouring for relevance in the decisional processes and the actual 'little' (and sometimes frightening) revolts of civil society have induced a sense of urgency in the process of decentralisation of authority and devolution of power. Several states have begun again the process of public review of their constitutions.

So, basically, there are two issues. The first questions the nature of the contributions of the state, local government, and non-state sectors to a new system of governance which is decentralised, democratised and effective. The second is how, specifically, these attributes are to be combined to describe how all the Anglophone Caribbean states should be governed - nationally and regionally.

RELATIONSHIPS FOR GOOD GOVERNANCE IN THE ANGLOPHONE CARIBBEAN

The purpose here is to begin the process of linking central government, local government and non-state sectors (especially NGOs) in a relationship which conduces to good governance. The largest assumption is that civil society is emerging in all countries as a significant factor in good governance and macro-economic policy, and must be treated co-equally in the grand macro-development scheme of things. This implies the necessity to look at Caribbean institutional frameworks which do or do not promote this growing interdependence and develop the capacity of communities and groupings to contribute to the empowering of individuals within them so that poverty can be conquered and well-being achieved.

The understanding of good governance used here starts with the achievement of liberalisation, privatisation, deregulation, decentralisation, and deconcentration of power, and community participation and democratisation (in local, regional and central) government. It explicitly accepts the principle of subsidiarity (meaning sharing the decision load down below) and collaboration with international donors and non-governmental organisations. The only problem is the meaning and purpose of these expressions which vary depending on the macro-economic paradigm within which they are used. There is a preference for a paradigm which privileges social sector reform.

The task is to modestly begin to put together some starter proposals for adoption and adaptation by individual Anglophone Caribbean states given the diversity which exists even with this category of Caribbean states. It will certainly not be the case of one model fits all. It is not the case of merely having expanded democratisation for the sake of citizen participation (social and political). The society must be shown as well to develop economically and culturally. The first place to start is with the Caribbean commitment to public sector reform which began, with some degree of urgency and seriousness of purpose, in the 1980s. Within that framework of technical improvements of central government administration, and the corresponding drive for decentralisation of central government services, can be set the renewed interest in refashioning local government by some Caribbean governments and the developing cooperation between governments and the various groupings which make up the non-state sector.

ANGLOPHONE CARIBBEAN GOVERNMENTS' COMMITMENT TO PUBLIC SECTOR REFORM

During the 1980s, various efforts at public sector reform were attempted but the results were less than pleasing. Initially, most of these efforts were directed at reducing significantly the number of public sector workers. The destabilising effect of this was considerable. The Caribbean Centre for Development Administration (CARICAD) was set up by governments with financial and technical support coming from international agencies to give support to national efforts at training and to provide critical research. Reform units and Ministries of the Public Service were established in several countries.

The Fifteenth Meeting of the Conference of Heads of Government of CARICOM States in the Bahamas on July 6, 1993, endorsed a proposal for a Working Group on Public Sector Reform and Administrative Restructuring. The Working Group conducted a series of country missions, workshops, case studies and two Ministerial Consultations and Symposia during the period July 1993 to November 1994. Four major studies were examined: (1) Constitutional and Administrative Reform, (2) Human Resources Management and Development, (3) Policy, Management and Implementation Strategies of Privatisation and Divestment, (4) and Financial Management of the Public Sector.

It has now been fully accepted by all Anglophone Caribbean governments that comprehensive, concerted and sustained attention must be given to public sector reform. There is now sufficient research and political commitment to move to the technical aspects of reform. The reports are detailed and form a basis for the devising of action plans with the appropriate financial package to achieve significant public sector reform.

These, and other reports, are extremely valuable but have been very weak on issues of social sector and local government participation. Indeed, the social sectors and local government have had better treatment in development prescriptions arising out of reports commissioned by international financial and aid agencies in relation to individual Caribbean countries.

The Anglophone Caribbean governments would agree with Andrew Dunshire that 'we shall simply not cope with social change now, let alone in the future, if we rely on the railway for transport, the telegraph for communications, and bureaucracy for government'. A new system of governance is needed!

NGO/NON-STATE ACTORS AND LOCAL GOVERNMENT CONTRIBUTIONS

An understanding of the institutional framework related to NGO and local government activity is necessary. In examination of their structure, five types of systems have been identified: (1) quasi-international non-governmental organisations (QUINGOs); (2) quasi non-governmental organisations (QUANGOs); (3) NGOs/CBOs; (4) National and regional networks of NGOs; and (5) Local Government. For full comprehensiveness and of utmost importance, the incorporation of other non-state actors, especially business and labour, must be undertaken in an adequate model of new governance.

QUINGOs are seen to have achieved outstanding success in Caribbean countries in spite of obvious weaknesses; and elements of successful methodologies of poverty intervention strategies have been highlighted. The over-articulated governance which IFIs impose on their sponsored agencies and the disproportionate focus on accountability processes rather than missions betray a deep mistrust of autonomous agencies in the Caribbean. Those efforts which have adopted an explicitly community development approach such as that of the Futures Fund in Guyana have shown how some aspects of this problem can be solved. The ecological NGOs have achieved outstanding success in their collaborative efforts with stake-holders including the government. The highly acclaimed work of the National Commission on Self Help (NCSH) in Trinidad and Tobago shows the institutional capacity residing in Caribbean countries for successful work in poverty reduction on a broad community-wide and nationwide basis. It proves that collaborative work with central and local government, community groups, state corporations and the private sector can and do work very well, and relatively autonomously.

Some examples of other NGOs engaged in poverty relief and development activities, some explicitly economic, and others more social, though no less significant for poverty reduction, have been examined. Their successes and problems have been revealed. Along with those cases which dealt explicitly with groups in environmental protection, whose work positively impacted upon poverty reduction and community empowerment, lessons about collaborative management and co-production have been derived.

National and regional networks of NGOs abound and form an impressive institutional framework for interventionary activity at all levels of decision making and action in poverty reduction. The Caribbean Policy Development Centre's (CPDC) work in regional and international advocacy, and the work of its member organisations sub-regionally and nationally have been recognised by governments and by the CARICOM Secretariat. Yet work needs to be done in making comprehensive the regional and national coverage of NGOs/CBOs and in securing formal recognition from governments as part of the policy process.

The Caribbean local government system is inadequately developed despite the sterling efforts of the Caribbean Association of Local Government Authorities (CALGA) to ensure its spread and its legal and constitutional recognition and relative autonomy from central government. Local government is a critical dimension of a reformed system of governance and hence its development is urgent. Local government is well situated between central government and NGOs to play a meaningful role in community development and poverty reduction. Some of their community development activities have been illustrated, based on a collaborative management approach, which reveal willingness and a capacity to be the basis of a country-wide structured response to poverty reduction. It has been strongly emphasised that local government should not be bypassed in the rush to generate parallel organisations and popular institutions.

At a CALGA workshop in 1994, the role of the state in actively promoting collaborative management and co-production activities was stressed. A recommendation was made for the establishment of a Social Investment Fund overseen by a National Commission, with broad-based membership, to encourage national efforts at poverty reduction. Institutional strengthening and capacity building for national and regional NGOs, as well as for Local Government was proposed. Among other recommendations throughout a paper presented by the author is the notion that a legal and constitutional framework needs to be provided by the state and, through a system of reformed governance, the necessary autonomy for multipartite (including all the non-state actors) arrangements to function with the greatest efficiency and effectiveness.

Experience has shown that for local government authorities to make a meaningful contribution to good governance and community empowerment, Anglophone Caribbean models of local government should contain the following features:

1. have constitutional or legal status;
2. municipal and district councils be established as statutory corporations so that local authorities can act fully as development agencies;
3. meet the criterion of full electiveness;
4. have well-defined financial autonomy; and
5. explicitly establish local authorities as community development and empowering agencies as part of their constitutional and legal mandate.

Local government systems, where they exist, are closer to targeted populations, are in a position to strengthen what people already do to survive economic recession and structural adjustment, and can join with credit unions, trade unions, and NGOs in this common endeavour of empowering people. In this way they can prove to be effective instruments to work with the poor in communities to reduce poverty and generate work for people using local resources oriented towards the internal market and placing the unmet needs of the population of the locality or region in the centre stage.

The efforts of the poor and disadvantaged have often been limited or stifled by the lack of transfer of adequate technological progress to what they do. Local governments, through their connections with central governments, through their ownership and control of vital equipment and facilities, and through their elected representatives, are well placed to make themselves relevant in ensuring food security and the creation of economic productive environments.

Local government should not be bypassed in the generation of parallel organisations and popular institutions. They should be facilitated by constitutional, legal and institutional changes which promote decentralisation, devolution and democratisation of authority and power to be an integral part of the community development process. They are, increasingly, revealing the willingness and capacity to move firmly in this direction.

From a review of collaborative activities between local government and community groups it became obvious that communities were fully capable of identifying their own needs, planning how to meet them, and implementing the agreed plan. In doing so a variety of resources are mobilised which added tremendous value to the limited financial and material support provided by local and national government, other interest groups and the international community. If governments are prepared to tap into this dynamism and reservoir of effective governance, then considerable improvements can be made to the lives of people in a wide variety of ways.

ARTICULATING CENTRAL GOVERNMENT REFORM, LOCAL GOVERNMENT RENEWAL AND NON-STATE SECTORS IN A NEW GOVERNANCE SYSTEM

Although there has been the appearance of numerous NGOs in the Anglophone Caribbean, they do not, and must not be allowed to, supersede the role and function of local government, whether in a unitary system or as part of a federal government arrangement. More importantly, the responsibility of the state for social welfare and development must not be allowed to lose coherence. The power and authority of the state must, necessarily, be diffused to new centres of action closer to beneficiaries and involve the latter's meaningful participation at all stages; but the state remains central.

The reason is as simple as it is often overlooked in exaggerated views about what NGOs/non-state actors and local governments can do. None of these institutions (local government, NGOs/non-state actors) can, at any time, even with the most extensive and intensive capacity-building, be the agency through which the contradictions of planned change and induced development be primarily or ultimately addressed. It is in their interrelationship and shared, though not necessarily equal, responsibility, within the framework of a new system of governance, that a new synergy will be released, which will produce better development and better government.

NGOs/non-state actors and local government should not be seen as competing forces which are better able to put people at the centre of development. They must of necessity collaborate. The weaknesses of the one are oftentimes delicately offset by the strengths of the other. NGOs may be seen, as Annis (1987) noted, as small scale, politically independent, low cost, and innovative - as positive attributes.

However, these features are unable to cope effectively with pervasive poverty and dispossession. They are unable to offer a sustained and integrated assault, lacking institutional and financial connectedness to central government, and lacking a general base rooted in representative elections. NGOs, however, especially the grassroots organisations have a direct legitimate basis through their activities. Their experiences, shared with national and local decision-makers, provide invaluable lessons vital for conceiving development interventions. International donor agencies are rapidly learning this.

The same points can be made in relation to NGO/government relations and the two with local government and other non-state actors. Central government lends itself to macro studies, NGOs to micro studies (especially of the types adumbrated in this report) and local government lends itself to neither. These are very general statements to be sure but they contain essential truths. Local Government's location between community and nation leaves it well placed to bring civil society and Central Government together in urgently productive relationships. It has to be ensured that well-planned decentralising, devolving and democratising exercises are designed with the full participation of these three groups, with labour and business fully involved. These exercises must ensure that there are sufficient resources to enable local government and NGOs/community-based organisations to meet local needs for poverty reduction and social development.

NON-STATE ACTORS AT THE CARICOM, GREATER CARIBBEAN AND INTERNATIONAL LEVELS

The tremendous divergence and complexity of groups in civil society raise considerable doubts about their ability to come together and speak with a common voice on a range of issues.These fears of governments and regional secretariats of Caribbean organisations are legitimate.The only real answer is the widening and deepening of regional networks of non-state sector organisation based on the strengths of national integrative organisations.This would mean for the business groupings that they develop at the national level an umbrella organisation representative of all levels of national business groupings, which would then select representatives to regional representative bodies. It would help considerably if this process were systematic, transparent and democratic.The Caribbean Association of Industry and Commerce (CAIC), for example, in spite of its importance, and the excellent work it has accomplished at the regional level, cannot claim an organic linkage with all national business organisations in each of CARICOM's member states.

The Caribbean Congress of Labour (CCL) is the closest that the Anglophone Caribbean region comes to an omnibus organisation yet in its member states the Trades Unions Congresses or Councils do not necessarily embrace all the active trade unions in existence.To the extent that it is possible to do so, such organisations strengthen their legitimacy base.

The Anglophone Caribbean NGO movement has an umbrella organisation, the Caribbean Policy Development Centre (CPDC) which coordinates the policy and advocacy activities of most of the more well-known national federations of NGOs, yet there is significant membership deficit of other networks and the host of CBOs which are not part of networks. In addition, there are a host of 'professional' associations which should probably be comprehended under CPDC's framework for purposes of arriving at a non-business and non-labour perspective on regional and international issues from a civil society perspective. Conceptually, it is a monumental task and would require financial and human resources outside the capacity of existing active NGOs to accommodate. Nevertheless, there is an extent to which a 'network of networks' organisation such as CPDC should remain a relatively open organisation.

Ideally, these regional organisations should be enabled to host annual or biannual conventions to reach national and then Caribbean-wide consensus on a wide variety of issues from poverty eradication to trade to monetary union to cultural union, or whatever. At the national level a national forum embracing central government, local government, business, labour, NGOs/CBOs, the Church, professional associations and the like, could be the interlocutory space for the articulation and possible integration of different interests, which could then feed, in a predictable manner, into the policy process. Separately, and on some matters, collectively, this process could be replicated at the regional level in a general way, and in specific ways in relation to regional institutions. The Regional Economic Conference held in Trinidad in 1991 pointed to a general mechanism.

Regrettably, the more embracing Regional Social and Economic Conference promised by the Heads of CARICOM states to meet as early as in 1996 has not yet been held. To be really authentic, it would need to be preceded by consultations at the national level, and, before that, by national consultations among individual categories of interests in the non-state sectors and local government. Regrettably, too, the decision was taken in relation to the newly launched Assembly of CARICOM Countries Parliamentarians, to limit direct participation in its deliberations to Parliamentarians, with non-state sectors as observers. However, these point the way for the necessity to make the effort at regional integration as much a bottom up as a top down affair. Change and development from the 'bottom' requires change and development from the 'top'. The concertation of this project from both directions as well as horizontally among similar groups will determine the degree of success at regionalisation and integration for the Anglophone Caribbean countries among themselves and with the greater Caribbean.

Neville C. Duncan
June 1997

SELECTED REFERENCES

Annis, Sheldon, "Can Small-Scale Development be a Large-Scale Policy? The Case of Latin America", World Development, Vol. 15, Supplement 1987

Agarwala, Ramgopal & Schwartz, Pushpa N. with Ponchamni, Jean, "Sub-Saharan Africa: A Long-Term Perspective Study", The World Bank Resident Mission in China, May 1994

Baker, Peta-Ann, "Issues in the Process of Government/NGO Collaboration", ADA, Kingston, 1962.

Ball, Colin and Dunn, Leith, "Non-Governmental Organisations: Guidelines for Good Policy and Practice", Commonwealth Foundation, Marlborough House, Pall Mall, London 1995

"Building Consensus for Social and Economic Reconstruction", Report of IDB Pilot Mission on Socio-Economic Reform in the Cooperative Republic of Guyana, IDB, Washington, DC, 1994

Cernea, Michael M., "Non-Governmental Organisations and Local Development", World Bank Discussion Papers, 40, Washington, DC, 1988

Drucker, Peter F., "The Age of Social Transformation", Atlantic Monthly, November 1994

Dunshire, Andrew, "Modes of Governance", Modern Governance, ed. Jan Kooiman, SAGE Publications, United Kingdom, 1993

Commonwealth Foundation, The, Report of the Second Commonwealth NGO Forum, Wellington, Aetearoa, New Zealand, June 1995

Community and the Environment: Lessons from the Caribbean, No. 1, "Protected Areas and Community Management," PANOS Institute & CANARI, Vieux Fort, St. Lucia, 1994

Community and the Environment: Lessons from the Caribbean, No. 2, "Community Participation in St. Lucia," PANOS Institute & CANARI, Vieux Fort, St. Lucia, 1994

Duncan, Neville C., "The Status of NGO/Government Relations within the Caribbean", CPDC, Barbados, 1995

Duncan, Neville C., "Mechanisms of Impoverishment in the Anglophone Caribbean", FES/CPDC, Jamaica, 1995

Geoghegan, Tighe, "Community Management Through a Small Business Approach to Forest Conservation in Dominica", a paper presented at the IDRC Workshop on the Common Property Resources, Winnipeg, Canada, September 1991, CANARA, St. Lucia

Girvan, Norman, "Community Power", a paper presented to ADA/AWOJA/SAC Panel on Community Participation in Local Government, Kingston, Jamaica, February, 1995

Hilaire, Ernest, "Negative Sovereignty and the Caribbean", M. Phil. Thesis, Centre of International Studies, Cambridge, England, 1995

Human Development Report, 1994, UNDP, Oxford University Press, Oxford, 1994

Korten, David C. and Alfonso, Felice B., editors, "Bureaucracy and the Poor: Closing the Gap", Kumarian Press, Connecticut, 1983

Martin, Atherton, "The Role of NGOs in Caribbean Social Development," a paper presented at a Caribbean Symposium on Social Development, in Barbados, Consortium Graduate School, and ISER, Kingston, Jamaica, 1995

Meighoo, Kirk; Crooks, Donneth, and Girvan, Norman, "Empowerment and Social Development: Theory and Practice", a paper presented at a Caribbean Symposium on Social Development, in Barbados, Consortium Graduate School, and ISER, Kingston, Jamaica, 1995

Ragoonath, Bishnu, editor, "Strengthening Local Government", Report of Caribbean Local Government Workshop, CALGA Secretariat, Port-of-Spain, Trinidad, 1995

Stone, Carl, "Democracy and Clientelism in Jamaica", Transaction Books, New Brunswick and London, 1980

Walters, B.B. and M. Burt, "Integrated Management of Common Property Fuelwood Resources from Natural and Plantations Forests in St. Lucia", a paper presented at the IDRC Workshop on the Common Property Resources, Winnipeg, Canada, September 1991, CANARA, St. Lucia

Chairperson Judith Wedderburn delivers the welcoming address at the CPDC Forum On Alternatives, Trinidad & Tobago, 1995.

Organisations and social actors in the regionalisation process

Judith Wedderburn

Prepared by Judith Wedderburn for the International Conference 'THE SOCIOPOLITICAL AGENDA FOR THE CARIBBEAN BASIN'S INTEGRATION PROCESS', INVESP, Caracas, February 12-13, 1996.

Judith Wedderburn is a Jamaican social activist, economist and director of the Friedrich Ebert Siftung's Jamaica office in which capacity she has edited a number of publications on developmental issues. She has conducted research on the Impact of the Globalisation Process on the Foreign Policy of Jamaica 1989 - 1992 and is currently researching the Impact of the North American Free Trade Agreement on women in Jamaica. Ms. Wedderburn has strong links with the NGO sector, serving as Deputy Chairperson of the Association of Development Agencies (ADA) and Coordinator of one of the programme areas of Women's Media Watch Jamaica.

Introduction

> 'The idea of a partnership in the exercise of political power to manage national affairs is gaining currency throughout the developing world. And the partners that are said to be vital to the new configuration of public management in the pursuit of better economic and development performance, are firstly, Government comprising accredited representatives of people who elect them via free, fair and frequent elections; secondly, the private sector comprising not only employers and managers of enterprises in the production process but also workers and their trade unions and associations; and thirdly, community organisations including the NGOs so designated and acting as hub in a network of voluntary citizens' groups committed to community action as a modality of development.' (Nettleford, 1992)

This quotation is taken from the preface of a publication based on the interventions made by Caribbean non-governmental organisations (NGOs) at a CARICOM Regional Economic Conference held in 1991. The history of the wider Caribbean is not replete with recorded attempts by social actors (interpreted here to mean institutions other than those in the government, the trade union or private sectors), to take a pro-active role in the Caribbean development process generally, and specifically in the regional integration process. This occasion in 1991 was, therefore, of great significance for Caribbean NGOs. This was the first recorded experience of a group of Caribbean NGOs who worked together to begin the process of positioning themselves as 'social partners', and intervened in the CARICOM regional integration process in a deliberately, structured and effective, although limited, way. Caribbean trade unions and the Caribbean private sector have long been recognised as social partners by CARICOM governments, and, as a result, had been previously accredited with 'joint consultative' status, through the Caribbean Congress of Labour and Caribbean Association of Industry and Commerce, respectively.

It is acknowledged that in the past five years a number of regionalisation initiatives spanning Latin America and the Caribbean have taken place. However, with the exception of the recent formation of an Association of Caribbean States (ACS), these initiatives have for the most part focussed primarily on Latin and Central America and paid scant attention to the Caribbean as a distinct entity. For the purposes of this paper, therefore, the Caribbean Basin (or the wider Caribbean) is taken to include Cuba, the Dominican Republic, Haiti and Puerto Rico along with the fourteen member states of CARICOM, established by the Chaguaramas Treaty in 1973. The Caribbean is recognised as a region with distinct cultural, social and political characteristics, an entity unto itself, not to be subsumed under a larger Latin American region.

Preparatory documents to the CARICOM Regional Economic Conference 1991, note that in reaction to the threat of further marginalisation by the current globalisation process, 'the Caribbean Basin countries have initiated a process of regionalisation through the promotion and establishment of intergovernmental trade and economic co-operation initiatives such as the Association of Caribbean States. However, this is mostly a governmental trend basically related to the initiatives of political and economic elite, with an emphasis on state and private sector action.' This process has created the conditions for the emergence of a regional civil society through the action of different NGOs, social movements and social organisations. The documentation also acknowledges that 'there are no institutional provisions in the ACS or other sub-regional integration schemes for implementing the participation of these actors in the regional integration process.'

This critique of the ACS supports the view of Guyanese Professor Clive Thomas (1979) who, in analysing the reasons for the failure of the old West Indies Federation, notes three lessons to be learnt:

- first, a region cannot be integrated from above, by simply proceeding to bring together the existing governmental structures;
- second, the approach to integration cannot be one that sees integration as an administrative convenience;
- third, the capacity for effective regional integration of the Caribbean ultimately depends on the degree of development of internal political and social forces in the region. These can only be measured by the extent to which the basic class interests of all working people, indigenous peoples, small farmers, women and youth are able to influence or dominate the social and political processes of development.

Later attempts at regional integration through CARIFTA (1968) and CARICOM (1973) were restricted to pragmatic forms of economic and functional co-operation suggesting that the major actors in the formation of these two regional institutions continued to view the process of regional integration simply as a means to an end but never as an end in itself. Ian Boxill (1993) concludes that as a result 'the Caribbean regional integration movement is weak and unstable because it is not based upon, nor is it guided by, an ideology of regionalism'. The pragmatism of the economic and functional co-operation which were the driving forces behind the CARIFTA/ CARICOM type of regional approach did little to foster the development of those internal social and political forces which could lead to some kind of ideological consensus that could inform the integration process.

Rather, the elite domination of social, political and economic institutions resulting in their hegemony over the masses of people, the relationship between the Caribbean elite and foreign capital, the manner of insertion of Caribbean economies into the hemispheric and global economy have mitigated against the development of effective mechanisms which would allow for the continuous interaction of people from historically insular countries.

This comment applies equally to the countries of the Spanish-, French- and Dutch-speaking Caribbean.

Present institutional mechanisms either in CARICOM or the ACS do not allow for the effective representation of, or intervention by, Caribbean civil society, (although the situation in CARICOM could be remedied in the near future). There is a growing recognition throughout the region of the increasing danger of political instability, of increasingly ineffective modalities of governance, of rapid deterioration in the environment and in the quality of life of the majority of Caribbean peoples. It is against this background that the role of Caribbean NGOs, working through the Caribbean Policy Development Centre (CPDC) will be briefly described, with a concluding analysis on how the interests of a regional civil society might be best served through the regionalisation process.

CARIBBEAN NGOS IN THE REGIONALISATION PROCESS

The term 'NGO' is sometimes used very loosely in the Caribbean to refer to any organisational form that is not governmental, or part of any state structure. It is also sometimes used to refer to a specific type of civic or social organisation. For the purposes of this discussion, it is used in its broadest sense: as a non-state entity it is a development-oriented organisation whose mission is centered on impacting on the quality of life of people in communities, or centered on effecting meaningful change in a particular sphere of social or economic life. The Caribbean Policy Development Centre (CPDC) could be properly described as a networking NGO since it comprises a number of NGOs that have identified common needs, and have agreed to combine efforts around a common agenda in order to maximise their impact.

CPDC was established in February 1991 as a regional structure aimed at defining development alternatives for Caribbean society and at working towards the formulation and implementation of 'policies which are in the interest of Caribbean people'.

Caribbean NGOs as represented by the CPDC are informed by an approach which identifies systemic factors as causing the inequality and exploitation that marginalises various groups within society. This approach also identifies with 'a development philosophy that addresses the human need for a sense of identity, community, spirituality as well as basic material needs' (CPDC, 1992). This view of development sees the production of material things not only for the purpose of capital accumulation, but primarily for increasing human dignity.

In addition, the approach recognises and promotes the richness and creativity of a Caribbean that is unique in its cultural, ethnic and religious diversity. Any programme of regional integration will therefore be a component of 'an alternative model of development that is grounded in the concerns, needs and aspirations of the region's people' (CPDC, 1992). The building of consensus; an insistence on a participatory approach to programme design and implementation; research, and public education and advocacy with a focus on popular methodologies are integral parts of the CPDC approach which seeks to build the confidence and ability of Caribbean peoples to influence public policy.

The present membership of the CPDC comprises twenty-one NGOs that are either regional, sub-regional, or national networks, or national agencies with a regional perspective. CPDC's geographic scope is defined as encompassing all of the major language areas of the Caribbean - English, French, Spanish, Dutch and Creole. Currently, members are present in all language areas of the region except the Dutch Caribbean. Member agencies in the Dominican Republic, Cuba and Haiti constitute an essential geo-political relationship that creates several new challenges and opportunities for English-speaking NGOs.

One of the main reasons for the establishment of CPDC is stated very clearly by the former Co-ordinator: 'a concern by the groups on the ground with the impact that the structural adjustment policies of the Bretton Woods Institutions was having on the livelihood of people at the level of communities, and a feeling that people did not fully understand where these policies were coming from, what they meant, and what could be done about them. So that the first task of the CPDC was to seek that information, to inform, and to advise, and to bring to that process the experience of these organisations on the ground to define our response to those policies'.

Collectively the member agencies of the CPDC bring together NGOs which work with and represent a wide range of interests in civil society. These include rural development agencies, church (ecumenical) agencies, women's groups, youth groups, popular theater workers, economists, media workers, human rights organisations, farmers and indigenous peoples. Through extensive research and documentation by its own member agencies, and informed by other work done regionally and internationally, the NGOs are of the view that the present economic and societal crisis in the region has its roots in the structuring of these economies during the colonial period to be producers of goods for export and to be importers of consumer goods. This historical pattern of underdevelopment continued into the post-colonial period and contributed to the region's increased vulnerability to the world-wide economic downturn of the 1970s and 1980s. Judging from the regulations and provisions of the GATT and the WTO, the contemporary situation, rather than envisioning the possibilities of a more humane, sustainable and holistic development effort for the region, suggests a period of recolonisation.

At the opening of the Regional Economic Conference, Peggy Antrobus (1991) noted the following: 'While analyses at the official level acknowledge the dependency of our economies on the dominant economies of the world system, our policies of export-oriented, foreign investment-dependent production seem designed to intensify this dependency, to lock us more firmly into a world-system in which market forces determine everything.' What this means in the current phase of the globalisation process is that the deepening relationship of interdependence which characterises international relations is not mutually beneficial to all the countries involved. Neville Duncan (1995) notes: 'The concept of recolonisation is used here because all of these processes (NAFTA, GATT, AFTA) have one, and without fail, one result - the maximum and the most efficient and most subtle extraction of surplus value away from poor and weak countries to the rich, in particular G-7, countries of the world.'The negative impact of post-colonial development strategies on the peoples of the region has been well documented. What has not been so well documented are the creative responses and survival mechanisms at the level of households, communities, districts and countries across linguistic boundaries.

Duncan (1995) expresses this sentiment in another way: 'Civil society has been revolting and new modus operandi and new institutions have been emerging. There has been a shifting of the balance between government and society away from the public sector and more towards non-state actors'. This has produced new patterns of interaction between government and society and can be observed in areas such as social welfare, environmental protection, education and physical planning. To give concrete expression to such new patterns of interaction, and informed by its commitment to bring the experience, the creativity and energies of the main actors of civil society to bear on policy responses, the CPDC has sought to have Caribbean NGOs recognised as one of the three social partners, and given joint consultative status within CARICOM along with the trade unions and the private sector.

Towards this end, an advocacy tool in the form of a document entitled 'The Status of NGO/Government Relations within the Caribbean Community and Recommendations for Improvement' was commissioned by CPDC, and produced (June 1995) after a process of consultation and review by the membership. Interventions by a team of CPDC members at the Heads of Government Meeting in July 1995, and submission of this document resulted in the Heads agreeing that the NGO community should be represented in the Joint Consultative Group as a body. However, the Heads are still to confirm that this NGO body should be the CPDC.

At the sectorial level, it is also possible to demonstrate how the CPDC through a member agency was able to successfully represent the interests of an important constituency within civil society, that is, Caribbean women. Reference is made here to the work of the Caribbean Association for Feminist Research and Action (CAFRA). Based on its regional work on 'Women and the Law', CAFRA was invited to join the Women In Development Desk of CARICOM in their governmental/NGO meetings to develop the model legislation. CAFRA also played a pivotal role in relation to the Beijing Conference. As a regional network, it was appointed as the NGO focal point towards Beijing, and was also invited to the 7th Meeting of CARICOM Ministers with Responsibility for Women In Development in May 1995. There the organisation presented a 'Briefing Document on the Fourth World Conference on Women', and used the opportunity to propose that certain actions be taken by Caribbean governments.

Other CPDC member agencies such as the UWI's Women and Development Unit (WAND), the Association of Development Agencies (ADA), the Caribbean Conservation Association (CCA) and the Caribbean Network for Integrated Rural Development (CNIRD) have taken the lead in various national, regional and international consultations and worked with the CARICOM Secretariat and member governments on many occasions. These NGOs, drawing heavily upon supporting donor agencies and upon their own limited resources, hired consultants, reflected upon their direct experiences in the field, analysed critical and urgent issues, and produced consensus papers, which were then used as advocacy tools in the appropriate fora. In these ways, they were able to make timely and relevant interventions even while other social partners (business and labour) floundered or became bemused by rapidly emerging challenges (Duncan 1995)

In summary, the CPDC has been able to respond very effectively to the regional conjuncture by articulating well-developed advocacy positions through which the interests and concerns of the major constituents of civil society were represented. These include:

- The Regional Economics Conference of 1991
- The West Indian Commission
- The Summit of the Americas
- The World Summit on Social Development
- The UN Global Conference on the Sustainable Development of Small Island States
- The Fourth World Conference on Women
- Lobbying the European Parliamentarians through KAIROS Europa.

Across the Caribbean, the form and content of such responses and mechanisms have been shaped by a number of different factors. These include the specific cultural, ethnic and religious impacts of different colonial powers, the pace and severity of stabilisation and adjustment policies, developments in the regional and hemispheric economies, the manner of insertion of the Caribbean economies into the global economy and the determination and commitment of the NGO leadership to utilise a Caribbean/regional approach to the issue of policy and development alternatives. In addition, the universal applicability of the regulations of more recently-developed institutions such as the GATT and the WTO have begun to have far-reaching effects on some of the more vulnerable local industries such as dairy and poultry in some countries, and would have added some urgency to the search for appropriate policy responses.

These Caribbean NGOs can be described as taking a pro-active leadership role in the process of regionalisation or advancing the regional integration process at a level other than the governmental. A question that needs to be asked, however, is: 'To what extent is the question of a Caribbean or a regional identity related to the regionalisation process?' Ian Boxill (1992) in examining the role of ideology in promoting regional integration suggests that strong national identities co-exist with a weak Caribbean identity, and identifies five characteristics of this identity with the greatest degree of support for common culture. Boxill also concludes that the regional integration process, albeit based on the CARICOM model, is unstable primarily due to this absence of an ideology of regionalism. Although Boxill's research was conducted only among the elite of two English-speaking Caribbean countries, and while advising caution in generalising from the findings to the entire region, he suggests that it is improbable that mass attitudes will be significantly different from those found in the survey, given the similar hegemonic position held by the economic, social and political elite in most countries. A related question which must then be asked is whether favourable conditions do exist for the emergence of a regional civil society?

Very briefly, Boxill concludes that: 'the data discussed suggest that there is some amount of shared ideas about the region among the elite of the two countries. However, these ideas are very diffused, and point to a weak regional identity. At the national and elite levels, these ideas are more cohesive and structured for each country, thus indicating stronger national identities.'

It has also been argued that a factor which contributes to the weak regional identity and to the non-existence of an ideology of regionalism relates to the negative way in which people perceive the region. According to Demas, what the region lacks is 'the kind of identity that goes with self-confidence; the kind of identity that generates a feeling of self-respect, self-worth and more dignity on the part of the people'. (Demas 1974) While such feelings may be identified as the product of the region's colonial past, and a tutelage which asserted that 'the best always came from outside', it is reinforced in the current era by North American entertainment, advertisement and news which now dominate the Caribbean media.

CHALLENGES FACING CARIBBEAN NGOS

The World Bank and other international lending agencies are now fully aware of the performance lapses of Caribbean governments. Large sums of money have been known to disappear in questionable if not downright fraudulent mis-spending due to political patronage and inefficiency. At the same time NGOs for the most part have been able to demonstrate through their own work that they can identify the real needs of people and, often in partnership with community-based organisations, contribute to development of meaningful programmes and projects.

As funding sources get scarcer, some international lending agencies such as the World Bank are now realising that NGOs can do a more effective job than governments in terms of implementing programmes and projects that benefit society's most vulnerable groups. The region's governments and the World Bank are now courting NGO alliances and advocating partnerships with NGOs as the way forward. The pressure and the temptation to access some of this newly available funding, despite some dangers, are now much greater for NGOs. In addition, some international financial institutions have successfully co-opted NGO methodologies such as participatory planning and research, and have incorporated them into their work styles and programmes. In response, NGOs have to become more focused, refining their practice and strengthening the theoretical and analytical basis of their work.

Regional economic conditions have had an impact on the nature of political development in the Caribbean to such a degree that the economic deterioration has been accompanied almost simultaneously by an increasing lack of interest in dominant political parties, and a growing cynicism that governments are no longer the main avenues for expressing demands and presenting alternatives. This has led increasingly to problems of governability, including non-participation in decision-making by the main actors in civil society, of legitimacy and of political stability. This has also led to a growing belief that NGOs can now become that vehicle through which satisfactory participation of people in the decision-making process at community, national and regional levels can be achieved, and through which civil society at the national level can be consolidated, and at the regional level encouraged to emerge.

A number of challenges for NGOs immediately come to mind while they seek to consolidate and more effectively provide for the representation and participation of civil society.

The need to work constructively with governments to design and support policies which benefit and improve the lives of Caribbean people, without facilitating the governments in their abandonment of the responsibilities to the populace by putting NGOs in 'the scapegoat position.'

While acknowledging that the responsibility for decision-making rests with the democratically elected governments of the region, the critical importance of ensuring that the views of NGOs, through CPDC, are considered equally with those of other social partners in discussions on issues of strategic importance to the region.

In the face of a dominant model that emphasises the primacy of capital accumulation over the non-material, social, cultural and spiritual aspects of human development, the challenge is to build the confidence and ability of Caribbean people to influence public policy in the direction of a holistic, people-centered alternative approach to development.

Remain appropriately humble and self-critical of the inherent weaknesses and contradictions within the NGO movement, and concentrate on maintaining a clear and focused organic relationship with the mass of people through community-based organisations.

Demonstrate the capacity of the NGO movement to articulate social demands from the perspective of empowering those seeking them, i.e. the main actors in civil society at national and regional levels.

Challenge the recolonisation of the region under the guise of generous funding for vulnerable economies, which will require that Caribbean NGOs work hand-in-hand with governments and funders, and yet not unwittingly be party to a process in which economic colonisers, acting as funders, gain even greater control over Caribbean countries.

Build dialogue across sectors (women and youth), between organisations (NGO-NGO or NGO-CBO), across language barriers and beyond the hegemony of the English language into a wider Pan-Caribbean vision in which the search for a more meaningful unity in diversity, and the effort to construct appropriate mechanisms to sustain that enterprise become a strategic imperative.

As these challenges are confronted, and the experiences, energies and creativity of Caribbean people through NGOs and CBOs are brought to bear on the process of identifying policy responses, and charting the way forward, the region should be one step closer to a regional identity around which the regionalisation process and a regional civil society could be mobilised. Rex Nettleford (1993) notes that 'despite the plurality of political systems and social orders, the various Caribbean territories find common bonds in that historical experience of resistance to slavery, colonialism and economic exploitation, as well as in the aftermath of that experience indicated in racism, intellectual dependency and the on-going need for economic and cultural survival in a world that was never really organised for the sort of existence created at the Caribbean crossroads.' The Caribbean then, is best acknowledged as a crossroads, a meeting place, and a centre of encounters of myriad cultural elements as well as a crucible in which new forms of human expression have been forged over this past half a millennium and are still being forged. These new forms of human expression, inclusive of a regional identity, will be important and critical components of any emergent regional civil society.

We end where we began by emphasising that the capacity for effective regional integration of the Caribbean ultimately depends on the degree of development of internal political and social forces in the region. To the extent that any emergent regional civil society is representative of the appropriate and necessary level of internal cohesion, to that extent a regional civil society will become a driving force in the regionalisation process.

Public forum to report on the United Nations Conference on Environment and Development, Barbados, June 1992. Dr. Peggy Antrobus is at left.

Towards a vision of the future: gender issues in regional integration

Peggy Antrobus

Andaiye

Andaiye has worked since 1987 as a resource person on gender and development. Between 1987 and 1993, she was employed mainly by the Women and Development Unit (WAND) of the University of the West Indies, where she facilitated theory-building and edited and co-edited theoretical papers. From late 1993, Andaiye's main attachment was with the CARICOM Secretariat where she was first a resource person for the Caribbean preparatory process for Beijing, and briefly, special adviser to the CARICOM Regional Post-Beijing Plan of Action. Andaiye also contributed to the Beijing preparatory process as one of the drafters of NGO documents at regional and international levels and through presentations to NGO fora. One of her main areas of focus is women's unwaged work. She has written and/or edited several papers on gender in the Caribbean, writes a weekly newspaper column on women and gender issues, and is active in the leadership of a number of national, regional and international women's NGOs. In 1996, she received a Guyana National Award for her work with women in Guyana.

Peggy Antrobus was born in Grenada and educated in Grenada, St. Lucia and St. Vincent. She holds a degree in Economics, a Professorial Certificate in Social Work and a Doctorate in Education. She has worked with government and NGO Programmes in St. Vincent, Jamaica and Barbados. Since 1974, when she was appointed as Advisor on Women's Affairs to the Government of Jamaica, she has worked in the field of women in development. In 1978, she set up the Women and Development Unit within the School of Continuing Studies of the University of the West Indies and was its head until her retirement in 1995. She was a founding member of CAFRA and is committed to contributing to the building of the women's movement in the Caribbean.

From 1991 to 1996, she served as general coordinator of the network of Third World Women promoting Development Alternatives with Women for a New Era (DAWN), and continues as a member of the steering committee. Her recent work focuses on the impact of government policies on women and the ways in which these policies reflect global trends.

This article was prepared in November 1991 at the request of the West Indian Commission and it is to that extent dated. However, despite the fact that some of the information, especially the statistical data, is out of date, the broad statement and analysis are as relevant today as when it was prepared seven years ago. In fact, more so in that the need for the region to rethink its direction and development strategies is now even more urgent in the context of the new trade regimes and the power to the WTO. Although the paper was commissioned by the West Indian Commission, its content was almost entirely ignored in the final report. The Women and Development Unit of the UWI and another regional journal subsequently published the paper. However, the authors welcome the decision by the CPDC to include it in this publication as a way of extending its reach.

Andaiye,
Guyana

Peggy Antrobus,
Barbados

ACKNOWLEDGEMENTS
The broad outlines of this paper were produced at a brainstorming session on April 25, 1991 involving a number of regional women's activists and researchers (see appendix). Many of these were the same women on whose research the paper relies. Later, a draft was circulated among them and key amendments and corrections were submitted by Kathleen Drayton, Joycelin Massiah, Joan French, Rosina Wiltshire, Rawwida Baksh-Soodeen and Magda Pollard. Among women who had not attended the session, important amendments and corrections were also made by Cathy Shepherd and Roberta Clarke (Caribbean Association of Feminist Research and Action), Nan Peacocke (Women and Development Unit) and Cecilia Babb (Caribbean Policy Development Centre). The final drafting of the paper was done by Peggy Antrobus (WAND Tutor/Coordinator) and Andaiye (WAND Consultant), who are therefore responsible for its text.

Introduction

'When we focus on women we are immediately confronted with a multiplicity of interrelated issues. Culture, family, food, water, health, income, media, and other social, economic and political issues call for attention.'[1]

In the past 15 years, the activities stimulated by the UN Decade for Women (1975-85) have generated a wealth of data and an analysis of the situation of West Indian women, their concerns and priorities, and their contribution to regional development.[2] This paper draws on that experience.

During this period, a small but influential part of the women's movement in the region moved beyond issues of equality with men and the integration of women in development to a vision of the transformation of the Caribbean as part of 'a world where inequality based on class, gender and race is absent from every country, and from the relationships among countries'[3]. In the words of the Hastings declaration, which emerged from the 10th Anniversary celebrations of the Women & Development Unit (WAND) of the School of Continuing Studies, UWI: 'Ten years ago we were seeking recognition and integration. Today we are seeking transformation and emancipation.'[4]

But in a region alert to how the subordination of class, race and nation interacts in Caribbean underdevelopment, the view persists that gender is an unimportant and divisive consideration. Thus, as soon as 'the woman question' is raised in relation to regional development and integration three questions are posed:

1. What specifically do women contribute to the process of regional integration?
2. Why the focus on women as a group when West Indian women are in an equal position to, if not a better position than West Indian men; and when women are an integral part of all the issues of West Indian life?

3. Isn't the 'women's view' of regional development lacking in an understanding of the 'real world'?

Given the role that the Commission is expected to play in articulating to the West Indian people and governments an analysis of the regional situation, and a vision of the regional future, based on the experience of all the West Indian people, its report must include the gender perspective on the issues confronting the region. This paper seeks to contribute to this purpose by briefly addressing the questions posed above under the following heads:

1. Women and the popular process of regional integration.
2. The nature of gender inequality and how it retards West Indian development.
3. In support of gender equality: Recommendations for action.
4. Conclusion: Towards a vision of the Caribbean future.

1. WOMEN AND THE POPULAR PROCESS OF REGIONAL INTEGRATION

The nature and significance of women's contribution to the popular process of regional integration is readily understood if we look at it in terms of three relationships which women have been central to creating and nurturing: the transnational family, regional networks of inter-territorial traders, mainly in agricultural products,[5] and regional networks of women and women's organisations.

Rosina Wiltshire and Linda Basch have analysed the impact of migration on West Indian culture and institutions. While their study is specifically on migration from Grenada and St. Vincent and the Grenadines to New York and Trinidad, many of their conclusions are more widely applicable in the region. This is particularly true of their conclusions on intra-regional migration which, they find, 'has deepened and strengthened the historic ties of Caribbean people and provided a foundation, at mass level, on which regional integration can be firmly lodged.'[6] It is this history of intra-regional migration that has led to the creation of the transnational family at the heart of which are women.

The transnational family is a nuclear or extended unit, which spreads across national boundaries. Family functions such as decision-making and giving economic and emotional support are divided among its members. The decisions may include things as basic as where children should be educated and matters related to building or extending homes.

Migrants maintain greater contact with female relatives, particularly mothers and sisters, than with male relatives in the countries of origin, and women also receive more remittances than men: in the countries studied, 33% receive over US$1,000 and 10% over US$3,000 annually, compared to 10% and 2% respectively of the men. One probable reason that women receive more frequent communication and more remittances is the important role they play in caring for children and maintaining the family in a culture that defines home and family as women's business.

The importance of the transnational family to regional integration is threefold. First, it is the most basic expression of the oneness of the Caribbean: a characteristic of West Indian people is their multiple family links, and it is not uncommon for members of a single family to have several different West Indian 'nationalities'. The links extend beyond the West Indies to include countries in the wider Caribbean; for example, for geographical and historical reasons, Jamaica has strong family links with the non-English-speaking countries of Panama and Costa Rica.

Second, it is important in the contribution remittances make to survival and development in the countries of origin: Basch and Wiltshire found that most of the relatives remaining back home received some form of remittance, and there was little difference in the amounts coming from Trinidad and New York. These remittances are used mainly for consumption, and the authors debunk the frequently-made distinction between consumption and development by pointing out that where, as in this case, consumption means the provision of basic needs, this is the 'foundation (upon which) effective development can be launched... especially... where (as in much of the West Indies) natural resources are limited and human resources represent the central resource base.'[7] Practical experience shows that remittances are also used as seed money for small business ventures, for example, to buy a sewing machine or a licence for petty trading.

But as the study demonstrates, the existence of the transnational family is important in a third way: it facilitates the operation of a second network - a web of inter-territorial trade in agricultural goods - by providing the traders with a ready pool of consumers for produce from 'home' and with a base from which they can operate their marketing in the host territory.

Most of those involved in this inter-territorial trade in agricultural produce are women. For example, according to an ECLAC study, women are 'over-represented' among inter-island traders from St. Vincent and the Grenadines and represent 85-90% of traders from Tobago.' That study also identifies the geography of the trade:

The section of the inter-island trade in which women predominate is divided into two major geographical circuits: the upper circuit which includes Martinique, Dominica, St. Lucia and Barbados, and the lower circuit which includes St.Vincent & the Grenadines, Grenada, Tobago, Guyana and Trinidad. These circuits are not closed, at times some islands of the upper circuit enter the lower circuit and vice versa.[9]

There is also a circuit in the Northern Caribbean between traders from Jamaica who travel to Haiti and the Dominican Republic

What is becoming increasingly clear is the trade's economic importance. For one thing, it is important in size. For example, of the 46,521 metric tons of agricultural produce which St.Vincent & the Grenadines exported in 1985 the bulk was marketed regionally; and inter-island traders from the territory carry out 80-90% of inter-island trade.'[10]

Their strategic importance is not restricted to economics. Niala Maharaj puts it this way:

> 'With their ground provisions and governor plums and sapodillas, they have established the most rational form of economic cooperation in the Caribbean since the Caribs and Arawaks. Were it not for them, we would have been at the mercy of the import-export merchants who would have happily weaned us into a total dependence on Kellogg's and

> Kraft. It is not unrealistic to argue that some of us would have completely forgotten the taste of balatta and sapodilla and eddoes. And so, we would have been held hostage to the suppliers of foreign food. The hucksters have been guardians not only of our small reserves of foreign exchange, but the culture that is our only protection against re-colonisation.'[11]

However, women traders face a wide range of problems: they work under poor conditions, for long hours, taking high risks. They undertake trading transactions, particularly with small-scale farmers in remote areas of the country, helping to sustain this important sector of West Indian society. Their involvement in this type of activity must also create special stress on their families, especially their children; and they probably could not undertake it were it not for the network of family and friends who provide support in their absence from home and in the territories they visit. They manage to make the contribution they do to conserving foreign exchange in spite of the fact that 'they exist within the cracks of a system which favours foreign businessmen and locals who can claim that they can attract ... foreign exchange.'[12] Their initiative, determination and hard work - with little or no support from governments or appreciation from the broad mass of Caribbean people who benefit from their labour - have succeeded in promoting the goals of regional food security in ways in which the elaborate and costly Regional Food Plan and the Regional Food and Nutrition Strategy have failed to do.

West Indian women's experience of 'region' is an experience of the wider Caribbean: as we have seen, both the transnational family and the trader network include non-English-speaking countries of the region. Perhaps out of this reality, when they initiate regional organisations, they often attempt to cross language boundaries. This was as true for the Caribbean Women's Association (CARIWA), launched in 1970, as it was for the Caribbean Association for Feminist Research and Action (CAFRA) and Women for Caribbean Liberation (WCL), both launched in the mid-1980s. CAFRA has moved the furthest in this direction.

Even where the notion of region is defined more narrowly to embrace only the English-speaking territories, the degree to which West Indian women's organisations have developed a regional practice is significant. As one example, the survey of women's organisations in Barbados carried out by Kathleen Drayton for submission to the West Indian Commission - and which covered the broadest possible range of women's groups - reveals that all but two have formal linkages across the region[13]

The term 'popular process' is usually defined to exclude the activities of government institutions. For women's organisations in this region, however, the popular process of regional integration involves increasing collaboration, in several territories and at the regional level, between women's NGOs and government-established women's desks. It also involves networking between these two groups and the university-based women's programmes: WAND, the Women's Studies group at the University of Guyana, and the Women and Development Studies programme at UWI which links the work of ISER and WAND to the teaching programme of the university. Where the university programmes are concerned, collaboration is facilitated by the fact that they all have an orientation towards action. This is a self-evident point in relation to WAND, whose mandate is outreach, and which plays an activist role in supporting women's NGOs and communities, as well as in advocacy; but it is also true of the research and teaching programmes, which work to influence policy.

In relation to the collaboration between government desks and women's NGOs (which predated steps by regional governments to work with NGOs as social partners), Audrey Roberts points out that in certain conditions this can be a rich collaboration: looking at the relations between desks and NGOs in the Bahamas and Grenada, she suggests that they 'illustrate how a climate fertile for feminism plus the willingness of government machinery to respond to and support that climate can make for new and transformational roles for such machinery.'[14]

At one level, then, networking among women's desks, university-based programmes and women's NGOs allows these groups to identify issues on which they can work together. At its best, it allows them to bring the strengths of their different mandates into action.

Although, as we have pointed out, most 'national' women's organisations in the West Indies function regionally, there is an important difference between the regionalism of the older women's organisations and that of the feminist groups which have emerged in several territories, many of whose members are part of the English-speaking membership of CAFRA. For them, not only is the commitment to a regional practice a commitment to work across language boundaries; it also derives from a perspective which links women's emancipation to the transformation of the total Caribbean society:

> '... the incorporation of the word 'feminist' in our name claimed for Caribbean... women the right to focus on all the specific issues facing women in our societies: issues which span the range of the social, economic, cultural, political and sexual. In addition, for Caribbean feminism as we have sought to develop it, the emancipation of women and the transformation of exploitative social and environmental relations necessitated a clear challenge to the dominant world economic system and the development policies which

emanated from it.'[15]

Some of the national feminist organisations, like CAFRA itself, also consciously organise themselves across class, race and cultural and religious differences and work to confront the contradictions that arise in their internal relations.

In addition to the structured organisations and programmes that exist in the region, there has been real growth in informal networks, most of which are aimed at the self-organisation of 'victims' to address their situation. For example, concern about the impact on women of cuts in the health services and the increase in chronic diseases among women is leading to increased attention to networking around issues of health. Within this, steps towards the formations of a regional women's cancer network has been spurred by problems arising in areas of medical care which CARICOM governments have begun to regionalise without taking adequate steps to facilitate the free movement of people requiring such care. There is also a proposal for a network of women with disabilities.

A different kind and level of regional network should emerge from the activities of WAND over the next few years, during which the Unit plans to build on its work with individual groups and communities over the past thirteen years. The aim is to strengthen the links between them so that they can build networks of geographic and interest group 'communities' pursuing a self-reliant approach to development.

When we speak of the regional women's movement, we are identifying the complex interrelation of efforts through which women individually and collectively navigate social and economic problems. While this movement is in no way dependent on governmental support, women throughout the region believe it would be advanced if governments strengthened the national women's desks and the CARICOM women's desk. In fact, all women's organisations and programmes in the region are constrained, as women generally are, by a lack of resources and lack of access to policy-making. These constraints are largely due to gender biases.

2. THE NATURE OF GENDER INEQUALITY AND HOW IT RETARDS REGIONAL DEVELOPMENT

Gender may be understood as:

> '... a network of beliefs, personality traits, attitudes, feelings, values, behaviours and activities differentiating men and women... It is historical; it takes place within different...spheres such as the state, the labour market,

> schools, the media, the law, the family-household, and interpersonal relations...'[16]

However, it is not neutral: 'it involves ranking of traits and activities so that those associated with men are normally given greater value... and therefore the formation of hierarchies, in most societies is an intrinsic component of gender construction.'[17]

The asymmetry of gender relations is detrimental not only to women, but to men and children and therefore to social, cultural, economic and political development in the wider society. The negative effect of this asymmetry is reflected in phenomena as varied as the lack of respect shown to women, the pervasive violence which characterises human relations in the region, the irresponsibility of much of male parenting, attitudes to work and authority, women's lack of power to promote and protect improvements in social/human development, the invisibility of much of women's work, and the consequent inadequacy of our national accounting systems to reflect the true value of women's production and therefore, of regional production.

WOMEN'S DUAL WORK LOAD

Behind the gender hierarchies in society is the responsibility that women have for the unpaid and unacknowledged labour of housework, i.e., for the production and reproduction of everyone's labour power.[18] Given their dual roles in the household and workplace, women tend to work longer hours than men, the more so in the poorest communities in rural and urban areas, where the conditions under which domestic work is carried out are onerous and time-consuming. Yet these are among the women whose incomes are most essential for family survival and who are responsible for critical areas of economic production such as agriculture.

The intent and impact of the internationally-influenced policy of structural adjustment provide a clear example of the linkages between women's productive and reproductive function. The cuts in social services which are the centrepiece of this policy are based on a set of assumptions about women's roles, chief among which is that women are housewives whose time is infinitely elastic and therefore able to accommodate the additional demands placed on them by the need to fill gaps created by cuts in services. This policy reflects the view that it is possible to concentrate on economic production at the expense of the social sector. In fact, production and productivity are closely related to the physical, psychological and intellectual capacities of the labour force, all of which are largely determined in sectors - formal and informal - where, because of gender roles, women are the key actors. When, under structural adjustment policies, there is contraction in the social services, not only are women most directly affected both as employees and as users, but those on whose behalf they seek the services are also placed at risk, especially children and the elderly. Reports from several territories describe a frightening situation in the health services. A recent book puts the case starkly in relation to Dominica:

> 'Worsening health care services are one price the poor are paying for structural adjustment. The number of beds in the country's main hospital was reduced by 21 per cent from 1978 to 1987 ... Doctors at the Princess Margaret Hospital report constant shortages of essential supplies, forced by strict new budget controls. Cloth dressings must be used and recycled, and surgical and other wards have been combined. As a result, said one physician, "a child who comes in for a circumcision is very likely to leave with measles or another infectious disease and come back sicker than before".... Badly overworked nurses in Dominica's clinics and hospitals have left in droves....'[19]

If structural adjustment policies are predicated on certain attitudes to women's time and labour, a different approach would reveal that women's role in reproduction gives them a location from which they can play a unique role in addressing some of the major problems facing West Indian society, provided they are part of creating the policies and plans for such action. If this is not done, the effect will be to further increase their workload.

Housework is often dismissed as isolated and isolating work from which women need to be 'liberated' into real production. In our view, not only are women in their reproductive role a central part of production, but housework in the conditions of poor communities in the West Indies is not work which takes place mainly in the confines of the home. Many of its tasks require long hours outside the home and involve networks of mutual support which women create to assist them in managing their workload. These tasks might include fetching water, washing clothes or marketing, for example. The more difficult the conditions, the more marked this tendency becomes: Guyanese women from poor communities spend hours each day, in the company of other women, buying food, and they organise to reduce the time and energy they expend on this task by exchanging market information among themselves and making purchases on behalf of each other. While the circumstances under which the women perform this aspect of 'housework' are clearly burdensome, they help make the community - as an extension of the household - a collective workplace in which consciousness of a shared condition grows and the women develop organisational capacity. One wider area in which this skill can be applied is in disaster preparedness and rehabilitation: the experience of Hurricane Gilbert in 1988 in Jamaica demonstrated that community organisation was a critical factor.

WHY WOMEN'S WORK IS LOW-PAID

Women's work in the social services, including domestic labour, is mostly an extension of what they do in the home without pay and is therefore generally low-paid. The underlying assumption is that work that is done without pay in the home has little value done outside the home. Besides, women are regarded as secondary wage-earners who only work to supplement the male breadwinners wage: this in a region where 32% of households are headed by women, and which has little historical experience of women as 'housewives' - either among early Amerindian women or the women who later came to this region as enslaved or indentured labourers.

The segregation of women in low-paying jobs has been well-documented. For example, according to the 1980 Population Census in Guyana, while women represented only about 1/3 of the employed labour force, almost as many women as men worked in the categories of Professional and Technical workers (a category which includes the 'female' professions of nursing and teaching) and Clerical and Related Workers. In contrast, the ratio of women to men in Administration and Management was 1:7.[20] Even in teaching, an area that women are said to dominate, they are in a minority in decision-making positions. In Jamaica, for example, while two-thirds of the teaching staff at the secondary school level are women, two-thirds of all principals are men.[21] Similar statistics have been found in other territories of the region.[22]

Labour force statistics do not reflect work in the informal sector of the economy. This sector has grown with the contraction of the formal economy in many of the countries of the region, especially in Jamaica and Guyana. Indeed, in Guyana it is understood that the informal sector or 'underground' economy provides incomes for the majority of the population - 60% according to a report by the Inter-American Development Bank.

Women's preponderance in this sector reflects both their determination to secure a living for themselves and their families, despite the odds of an inequitable and harsh economic environment; and the high level of unemployment in the female labour force in the formal sector - almost twice as high as male unemployment in most countries in the region. Activities in this sector are indicators of the resilience, resourcefulness and self-reliance of West Indian women - qualities greatly needed if the region is to emerge from the ongoing crisis.

Data from Jamaica provide an example of the inequity between men and women in their access to income:

- Women's unemployment rate is more than twice as high as men's for all age groups. 70.29% of females between 14-19 are unemployed, as compared to 33.8% of males, while in the 14-24 age group the rate for women is 27% compared to 12% for men. 16% of female-headed households are unemployed.
- 41% of female-headed households earned less than J$200 a month compared to 15% of those headed by men. Almost half of all employed women are in low paid jobs and are either self-employed or work in the service sector (the two main categories being higglering and domestic work). The average wage for employed males exceeded that for females by 27- 47% during the period 1983-85.
- 60,000 women work in agriculture - representing 17% of the total female labour force and 20% of all farmers; yet 64% of women in agriculture have less than 1 acre of land or no land at all, and only 1% of loans from the Agricultural Development Bank go to women farmers.[23]

The situation of women in other member states is similar to that in Jamaica. In Grenada, for example, a female head of household earns an average of $200 a month less than a male head of household.[24] In the area of agriculture, a 1987/88 study on Women in Caribbean Agriculture (WICA) conducted by CAFRA in Dominica and St. Vincent showed that despite some variations, women's access to land is mainly through men; and while ownership of land in both countries is low overall, it is higher for males than females (in St. Vincent only 17% of the female sample owned land). Further, the inequitable distribution of land access between males and females is also reflected in government Land Reform programmes and in access to the use of Crown Lands.[25] Yet women represent over 30% of the region's small farmers, and predominate in the production of food for the domestic and regional markets.

The low wages of women and their inferior access to material resources inhibit the development of the whole society, since, as the WICA project has confirmed, women's primary area of expenditure is on food, clothes, education and other basic needs of their children and other family members - i.e., on human resource development. Men, on the other hand, are inclined to tend to their own needs first and to concentrate on 'visible' areas of expenditure, i.e., material things. The quality of the human resources in any given society is therefore critically affected by the access of women to income and material resources.

SCHOOL AND MEDIA AS REINFORCERS OF GENDER HIERARCHIES

Gender hierarchies are reinforced by the school, among other agencies of socialisation. Several factors contribute to this, one of which is the kind of textbook used in our schools. In a recent paper, Kathleen Drayton described how these textbooks perpetuate gender stereotypes:

> 'School textbooks are a universal teaching tool and the knowledge in them is the knowledge considered legitimate. Much of the knowledge that is distributed through the schools system is contained in textbooks. In November last year (1989) I analysed all the English Language textbooks used in our schools and written for the Caribbean Examinations syllabus.These were all published since 1978. I found that in these texts overall 92.3 % of principal characters in text and illustrations were male.
>
> 'I found that the text showed males in 98.5% of all top positions and 93.8% of all higher professional and related occupations. I found that families were overwhelmingly nuclear with only four extracts presenting one-parent families. I found that male/female relationships were characterised by domination and control of one sex over another. These relationships were also all characterised by fear and distrust, which is represented as beginning in childhood. Overall, the textbooks, and these are the ones all children use since English Language is compulsory, do not present relationships where males and females mutually respect and trust each other and are interdependent and equal in status.'[26]

The media, too, are both product and producer of the inequality of women, which is built into the social structure. This has been illustrated by an analysis of the print media, which formed part of a March 1990 study on the Caribbean media. This study examined more than 26,000 news items in newspapers and magazines in Barbados, Jamaica, St. Vincent and the Grenadines and Trinidad and Tobago, and found that the number of stories about women and issues which affect them was consistently low in all four countries, with global representation of women in news amounting to no more than 6.2% of the total of 1,730 news items examined. Generally, the publications did not reflect the lives of rural and poor women, and the more blatantly sensationalist newspapers were among the publications with the highest quantities of news items about women in the global and local categories.[27]

THE LAW AND WOMEN'S STATUS

A widespread assumption in the region is that, whatever may be the case elsewhere, women in the West Indies are equal to men in law. However, in spite of significant changes during and since the Decade, women continue to be subordinate in this sphere. The notion of wives as property continues to inform regional law, as illustrated by the law in Jamaica where the husband of a woman who commits adultery can bring legal charges against the defiler and user of his property. No similar recourse is available to women.

Of the many examples of laws that treat women as a 'lesser breed', citisenship laws are particularly important to the issue of regional integration. While there have been changes in these laws in several territories in the last few years, the following are an indication of the situation which existed until (at least) 1986:

- In Antigua and Barbuda, Belize, St. Lucia, and St. Vincent and the Grenadines, only a man who was a citizen could automatically transmit citisenship to his spouse.
- In the Bahamas, Barbados and Jamaica, citisenship could be acquired from a parent who was (or could be) a citizen only if the parent was the father. The discrimination was removed by the fact that in special circumstances - including where the parents were unmarried - a woman could transmit citisenship to her offspring.
- In Antigua and Barbuda, the Bahamas, Guyana, Jamaica, and Trinidad and Tobago only the male, but not the female adopter in a joint adoption could transmit citizenship to a minor.[28]

Although legal reform has been an area of real movement in the region during and since the Decade, Roberta Clarke points out that indirect discrimination persists in laws which ignore the socioeconomic reality of West Indian women's lives.[29] She provides the following examples of such laws in the areas of labour, family and violence against women, which women throughout the region have identified as the areas in greatest need of reform.[30]

Labour: As many as 44% of women in some countries are household heads while in some, more than 80% of all births are to unwed mothers.[31] In spite of this, several territories have no laws granting women the rights to maternity leave and pay. (The exceptions are Barbados, Belize, Dominica, Grenada, Jamaica and Montserrat). Instead, women must seek these rights through collective bargaining agreements, a situation that renders them vulnerable since so many of them work in sectors that are under-unionised (or non-unionised), in labour surplus economies.

Family: The major reform needed in family law is in child maintenance provisions, particularly because the large numbers of women with sole responsibility for their children's upkeep bear this responsibility in conditions of high unemployment, low wages and poor state support for low-income families.

Violence: The private sphere - the household - is the place where women are most vulnerable to the power of men, a power that often manifests itself in violence. Yet governments are only beginning to produce legislation addressing the reality of domestic violence and to provide women with remedies. Rape in marriage where the parties are living together is not a criminal offence in any West Indian territory.

While there is clearly an urgent need for continued legal reform, proposals on how laws should be reformed are not always in the interests of women (or justice). For example, a recommendation made in Jamaica was that men be given equal rights to the property and income of females in the event not only of divorce but also of separation, although the situation of women remains fundamentally unequal to that of men as regards access to property, social responsibility for offspring and expenditure on child-care and household.[32]

HOW WOMEN'S LIVES ARE CIRCUMSCRIBED

Beyond the practical gender issues confronting women, then, there are strategic gender issues associated with women's capacity to influence policies. In general, gender hierarchies in the public domain replicate those in the household. The existence and effect of gender-based hierarchies in the household, the community, the workplace and the country not only constrain women's access to resources, limiting their productivity, but also undermine concepts of participation and democracy. Women are under-represented in decision-making processes at every level, even in organisations based on occupations in which they are a significant percent of the producers. In St. Vincent, for example, the Banana Growers' Association requires a farmer to produce and sell 62,000 pounds of fruit a year to be a delegate to its Annual General Meeting, and at least 125,000 pounds to be a nominee for the executive. Since most women are small farmers, this amounts to their exclusion from policy-making.[33]

Of all the manifestations of gender inequality, violence against women has provoked the strongest mobilisation of women in several territories in recent years. Part of the reason for this is the sheer prevalence of violence against women in the home and on the street, and of sexual harassment in the workplace. Reliable statistics on any of these forms of abuse are difficult to compile, but in a study among Indo- and Afro-Guyanese women, Basmat Shiw Parsad and George Danns found an extremely high incidence of domestic violence, with two out of three women reporting having experienced it in some form. In addition to using official statistics, the authors did a survey of 220 women from rural and urban communities, of whom 50% were known cases of wife abuse and 50% randomly selected.[34] In Jamaica, it is reported that a woman is raped every eight hours.[35]

Throughout this paper, we support our assertions by data produced (mainly) through the research of regional women. But there is another kind of evidence that women's organisations in the region have: the evidence that comes from the experience of their own members as women, and from the experience of the women around whom they live and with whom they work. In relation to the causes of male violence against women there is insufficient statistical evidence, but information gathered from experience, particularly by women's organisations which work on the issue of women and violence (for example, SISTREN [Jamaica], Red Thread [Guyana] and WAND), indicates that a major cause of domestic violence is men's response to what they perceive as inadequate attention to their needs: from food not being ready 'on time' to women's failure to respond to their sexual demands. When women attempt to assert themselves, the expectation of dominance into which men are socialised often leads to increased violence. Sexual abuse and violence in the workplace and on the street are a product of the same socialisation.

Violence directed toward women is therefore inherent in the conditions under which social organisation is maintained; and the consequence is that women's lives are often circumscribed by fear: from the fear of breaking out of traditional roles and being seen as a challenge to men and therefore unsuitable for partnership with men; to fear of exercising the simple freedom of going out alone, or even in groups, at night. This intimidation not only limits women's self-realisation but also deprives society of the fullness of their creative contribution to the development of society.

3. IN SUPPORT OF GENDER EQUALITY: RECOMMENDATIONS FOR ACTION

Women will not be able to make their full contribution to development unless they have control over their fertility, legal justice, equal access to skills and resources, and most importantly, real opportunities to participate in decision-making processes - at all levels - on the basis of their experience as women. This is a crucial point: too often we hear of the need to have 'more women in decision-making positions'. This is a necessary but not sufficient condition for enhancing women's unique contribution to society. The important question is whether their participation makes a difference to the process and types of decisions taken.

But in making the following recommendations, we have limited ourselves to areas around which both the consultative process of the Commission and the proceedings of the Regional Economic Conference (Trinidad 1991) have shown considerable consensus and have sought to integrate concerns of particular importance to women within them. These recommendations are therefore specific, practical and few in number. Many have a direct bearing on human resource development.

I COUNT WOMEN'S WORK

The consequences of gender inequality are reflected most glaringly in public policy and investment, preventing women from realising and performing to their full potential. The exclusion of women's unpaid work - in the household, subsistence agriculture, the informal sector, and the voluntary sector - from national income accounting makes the Gross Domestic Product (GDP) an inaccurate base for the calculation of economic policy. It might also be a factor in the neglect of subsistence agriculture and the informal sector - two areas of economic activity which have helped to sustain livelihoods in times of downturn in the formal economy, and which may serve as a basis for policies aimed at building self-sufficiency.

The invisibility of women's work and contribution to the national product also limits the options which governments may exercise in relation to international financial and development agencies: if a value were computed for women's contribution to GDP there would, perhaps, be stronger arguments for resisting demands for cuts in the services on which these women depend.

In 1980, the United Nations called on all governments to count the contribution of the unpaid work that women do on the farms, at home and in other fields. At the final World Conference of the UN Decade for Women in Nairobi in 1985, governments agreed that:

> 'The remunerated and, in particular, the unremunerated contributions of women to all aspects and sectors of development should be recognised, and appropriate efforts should be made to measure and reflect these contributions in national accounts and economic statistics and in the gross national product. Concrete steps should be taken to quantify the

unremunerated contribution of women to agriculture, food production, reproduction and household activities.'[36]

This was ratified by the UN General Assembly on 6 November 1985. To date, no CARICOM government has taken 'concrete steps' on this agreement.

II. TAKE CONCRETE STEPS TO COMBAT THE IDEOLOGY OF MALE DOMINANCE

The ideology of male and female sex roles is transmitted from one generation to the next through education. The present belief system enshrines male dominance. Governments should therefore support a three-pronged policy directed at three critical areas of education: the media, teacher education programmes and schools.

Media: Existing studies on the media should be used as a basis for the formulation of media policies which will address the exploitation of women as well as the transmission of the ideology of male and female social roles.

Teacher Education: Teachers are key persons in education: their influence reaches from children at the pre-primary age to adults of the post-primary stage. A compulsory component of all teacher education programmes should be gender education, and the University of the West Indies Women and Development Studies programme, along with Teachers Colleges and Ministries of Education, should be mandated to develop modules in gender studies appropriate to different levels of education and training.

Schools: We recommend as one specific, immediate area of action that governments support a project leading to the development of teaching materials free of gender bias for use at all levels of the educational system.

Secondly, we suggest that governments address the over-representation of men in the administration and management of education in schools.

Thirdly, we propose that governments support studies on the effects of coeducation on the achievement of boys and girls in schools.

III. PROVIDE TOOLS SO INSTITUTIONS CONCERNED WITH MONITORING THE STATUS OF WOMEN CAN CARRY OUT THEIR MANDATE

A commitment to redressing gender inequalities is meaningless unless national and regional institutions, which are concerned with monitoring the status of women and recommending policy, are given adequate tools. These would include:

- Providing adequate infrastructural support for national women's desks and the CARICOM women's desk..
- Formalising a consultative arrangement between CARICOM and women's organisations at the regional level.
- Regular collection and publication of sex-disaggregated national and regional statistics to provide more accurate data for development planning.

IV. SUPPORT THE INFORMAL SECTOR

Given the significant and increasing role in the economies of the region of the informal sector, a sector in which women are preponderant, urgent attention needs to be given to a consideration of the policies and institutional reforms which will support these activities without prejudicing the creativity of the people involved.

Traders represent one kind of activity within the informal sector, a sector which makes a significant contribution to the survival of large groups among the Caribbean people. This activity illustrates some of the complexities of the informal sector. It has been argued that there are indeed not one but many informal sectors including at least three types of activities: those related to the formal sector (e.g. subcontracting with a view to reducing overheads and cutting costs of production); secondly, small scale enterprises producing goods and services for lower and middle income groups; and thirdly, those engaged in petty self-employment. Traders are involved at all of these levels, although those in the networks we described earlier are mainly at the third level. There is need for research which will distinguish between the widely varying types of activities and the conditions within which the activities grow and for policies to be informed by the data generated by this research.

However, in the short run, there is also need to ensure that the problems faced by traders in agricultural produce (which have been well documented) are addressed. These problems include theft and spoilage of their produce because of inadequate infrastructural arrangements, and harassment by customs and immigration officials and handlers on the docks.

V REMOVE RESTRICTIONS ON FREEDOM OF MOVEMENT FOR CITIZENS INVOLVED IN REGIONAL INSTITUTIONS AN ARRANGEMENTS

We believe in freedom of movement for all Caribbean citizens. However, accepting that even in relation to the CARICOM countries a phasing-in process is inevitable, we nonetheless feel strongly that the list of those who will begin the process should not be limited to people defined as skilled.

Instead, in the interests of furthering a regionalism already in motion, it must include all CARICOM citizens who need to travel through the region as part of networks and arrangements that are in the regional interest. We identify these as:

- Inter-territorial traders, particularly in agricultural produce
- People who need to travel for health care or to accompany people needing to travel for health care
- People with direct family links - child, partner, parent, grandparent or other guardian - in other CARICOM territories; in other words, members of transnational families in the West Indies
- People working in regional non-governmental organisations and programmes, who should also be encouraged and supported by exemption from travel and departure taxes for travel to attend regional meetings or to undertake tasks related to regional development

Within the area of freedom of movement, we want to draw the Commission's attention to the scandalous treatment meted out to Rastafari and citizens of certain West Indian countries at many airports in the region, and to sound the warning that the movement to regional integration may be thwarted by the bitterness that is developing as a result of these acts of discrimination.

VI. CHALLENGE IMF STRUCTURAL ADJUSTMENT POLICIES

FIRST, TAKE A REGIONAL APPROACH TO NEGOTIATIONS

The Port-of-Spain Consensus, the final document which emerged from the Regional Economic Conference, calls for 'the region (to) speak with one voice on the issues which affect member countries in their relations with the outside world.'[37] An area in which it is urgently necessary for governments to strengthen their hand by taking a regional approach is in negotiating with the IMF, with a view to safeguarding the interests of West Indian people and creating the maximum room for manoeuvre in the evolution of long-term strategies for the development of the region.

SECOND, ALLOCATE SCARCE RESOURCES EQUITABLY

In the Port of Spain Consensus, CARICOM governments also agreed that 'the development of human resources will be assigned the highest priority in development strategies.'[38] As this paper has shown, a focus on gender issues points to the need to review and question the policies of structural adjustment, which have not only proved fundamentally detrimental to human development but self-defeating even to the narrower issues of human resource and economic development.

As we have suggested, structural adjustment policies, while ostensibly promoting productivity, destroy the very resources upon which this productivity depends. The ecological systems are endangered; the work of women increases; the health and educational status of the population deteriorate; malnutrition rises, especially among infants and mothers; crime and violence escalate; youth, alienated by neglect and hopelessness, turn increasingly to drugs; and migration becomes the escape route of greater and greater numbers of the region's people. As this process advances the political fabric of the society is dangerously weakened.

Given the critical impact of these policies on women and youth, it is important that these sectors be given priority in the allocation of scarce resources associated with IMF policies and the debt crisis. These sectors should also be central to the process and design of alternative long-term development strategies for the region.

In the allocation of scare resources, the principle of equity is important not only between groups but within groups - for example, between women of different classes. The allocation should therefore be directed at enabling the fullest participation of all in the development process, for their own self-realisation as well as the maximisation of national and regional development potential. In the context of Structural Adjustment Policies this will mean, among other things, ensuring meaningful access to capital, education, health services, and training opportunities for all those whose lives and livelihoods are under attack from the policies, with the greatest attention to those most affected.

THIRD, CONSULT THE PEOPLE

In keeping with the spirit of the Port of Spain Consensus, governments also need to implement processes of broad popular consultation and information-sharing, using appropriate and effective mechanisms. NGOs and all the social partners should be involved and governments should be guided by the views emerging from such a process in their dealings with the Fund.

4. CONCLUSION: TOWARDS A VISION OF THE CARIBBEAN FUTURE

What vision of an alternative has emerged from women's experience and the reflection which has been taking place within the regional women's movement?

Our vision is of a Caribbean integrated across language boundaries, including Cuba, in a world where men and women work to transform the relationships and structures that perpetuate the subordination of nation, class, race and gender and the exploitation of the natural environment

The first lesson we have learnt is the importance of a development strategy which is anchored to the goal of meeting the needs and aspirations of the region's people, and not merely of increasing profit for small sectors of the population of the North and South. The present development strategy widens the disparities between social groups and countries and breeds ecological degradation.[39] The model of development which has the market as the only engine of economic activity, in a relationship which functions in favour of the side which has the power, must be replaced with a model which puts people at the centre and therefore prioritises basic needs: in such a model, women will have a crucial place because of their role in providing basic necessities in both the productive and reproductive spheres.[40]

The present crisis 'provides an opportunity for real restructuring toward a more self-reliant, endogenous and participatory model of development'.[41]

The second lesson, then, is the importance of participation and consultation, and the need to locate these at the level of the community - community not only as geographical location, but as groups of people with shared interests: savings groups, sports groups, religious groups, trading groups, professional groups, women, youth, the aged, the disabled. The validation of these special interests is crucial to the redressing of imbalances within the society, the equitable allocation of resources, and a holistic and long-term vision of national and regional development.

Maxine Henry-Wilson has proposed that the paradigm of the community replace that of the market in an alternative model of development. She argues: 'The concept behind the paradigm which places the community as the focal institution of socioeconomic and political development relates to the need to redefine 'power' and to see these relations as mutual, complementary and transformative.

'A community by definition is a set of practices, institutions, behaviours and relations. All encounters are not based on exchange as in the market model. Rather, there are strong stimuli for mutual survival, for protection of each other for more cooperative relations. The two-person model of the market is replaced with interactions governed by shared values. Commodities do not become ends in themselves but means to achieve ends. These are the prevailing ethos that regulate community life.'[42]

Ultimately, West Indian governments and people must face the fact that equity must begin at the level of the household: the inequalities inherent in the sexual division of labour must be addressed if the region is to realise its possibilities.

Central to the issue of equity, too - at another level - is the need for change in the attitude of governments to the people, and especially to women. Governments of the region too frequently display contempt for the experience and intelligence of the people, withhold information critical to their participation in decision-making, and exclude them from the process of consultation which precedes major policy decisions. This political disempowerment is especially unfortunate since it is these very people who must bear the burden of unwise or failed policies, or who must ensure the success of wise ones.

In this paper, we have highlighted the contribution of West Indian women to strengthening the movement for regional integration. We have shown how women's central position is the family and their concerns for family relationships and survival have led them to build on relationships of kinship and friendship to establish networks for mutual support which have helped them cope with economic and social decline no less than with the vagaries of natural disasters. We argue that these networks can provide a sound foundation on which the more formal modalities of Caribbean integration might be constructed.

We have referred to the emergence of a regional women's movement which has moved beyond an exclusive concern for women to a concern about the quality of life for all Caribbean people, and whose work might lead to the growth of networks of self-reliant 'communities' of mutual interest and for mutual support. This movement is linked to a network of Third World women promoting Development Alternatives with Women for a New Era (DAWN) through which Caribbean women might contribute to the emergence of a new paradigm of development - one which more closely reflects the reality of the structured powerlessness of the economic South in relation to the North.

We have also explored the nature of gender inequality and suggested some of the negative consequences which follow from the asymmetry of gender relations in the region, not only for women but for the wider society. We assert that these consequences limit women's contribution to the realisation of a vision of the Caribbean, which is humane, equitable, self-reliant and sustainable.

We have suggested measures, which can be taken by CARICOM

governments, to strengthen women's contribution to regional integration. It is now for governments to demonstrate their support for the enterprise and initiative of Caribbean women by removing some of the continuing barriers to their contribution to the movement for an integrated Caribbean in the 21st century.

NOTES AND REFERENCES

1. Cuales. In Gender in Caribbean Development, p. 111.
2. In this paper, West Indies refers to the English-speaking countries of the region, Caribbean to the region across language boundaries.
3. Sen & Grown. Development crisis and alternative visions: Third World women's perspectives p. 80.
4. Hastings Statement of Women. In Report of the WAND 10th Anniversary Consultation and Symposium, p. 48.
5. Also called higglers, hucksters, traffickers and vendors.
6. Wiltshire and Basch. In Caribbean regional and international migration, p. 75.
7. Ibid, p. 63
8. Lagro. Women traders in St. Vincent and the Grenadines. Phillips. Women traders in Trinidad and Tobago.
9. Cuales and Lagro. Women traders in agricultural products, p. 5.
10. Lagro. Women traders in St. Vincent and the Grenadines.
11. Maharaj. In Fly-by-night traders of the Caribbean islands: do they hold the key to regional integration? p. 11.
12. Ibid, p. 11.
13. Drayton. Women's organisations in Barbados and regional integration.
14. Ingram-Roberts. The changing role of women's bureaux in the process of social change in the Caribbean, p. 8.
15. Baksh-Soodeen and Reddock. In Preface, Creation Fire: a CAFRA anthology of Caribbean Women's poetry , p. ii.
16. Berneria and Roldan. The crossroads of class and gender: industrial homework, subcontracting, and household dynamics in Mexico City, pp. 11-12
17. Ibid, p. 12.
18. Dalla Costa and James. The power of women and the subversion of the community.
19. McAfee. Storm signals: structural adjustment and development alternatives in the Caribbean, p. 116.
20. CARICOM. Women in Guyana: facts and figures.
21. Jamaica. Bureau of Women's Affairs. The National Policy Statement: the ten immediate policy goals and basic statistics, p. 5.
22. Drayton. The gender bias in education, p. 2.
23. Jamaica. Bureau of Women's Affairs. Op cit, pp 1 - 2.
24. Grenada. Department of Women's Affairs. Report on national symposium on the status of women, in Grenada, Carriacou and Petite Martinique.
25. Women in Caribbean Agriculture Research/Action Project.
26. Drayton. The gender bias in education, p. 7.

27. WAND. The involvement of Caribbean media in the implementation of the Nairobi forward-looking strategies for the advancement of women.

28. Caribbean Community Secretariat. Study to monitor the legal status of women in member states of the Caribbean Community.

29. Roberta Clarke. Memorandum to Andaiye and Peggy Antrobus.

30. As part of CAFRA's Women and the Law project, national consultations were held in Antigua, Dominica, Grenada, St. Lucia and Trinidad and Tobago. In these countries the participants reiterated what was also revealed in the ISLA/CAFRA survey on Women's Rights and the Law: that these areas represent the areas which immediately limit or facilitate women's social and economic development most profoundly.

31. ECLAC. Comparative status of women in selected Caribbean countries as indicated by selected social, economic, demographic legal parameters.

32. Recommendations of the 1975 Family Law Committee, Jamaica.

33. CAFRA. Women in Caribbean Agriculture Research/Action Project.

34. Danns and Shiw Parsad. Domestic violence and marital relations in the Caribbean: a Guyanese case study.

35. Jamaica. Bureau of Women's Affairs. Op cit, p. 3.

36. UN. The Nairobi forward-looking strategy for the advancement of women, p. 32, para. 120. The International Wages for Housework group and its affiliates have been spearheading a campaign to 'count women's work'.

37. CARICOM. The Port of Spain Consensus of the Caribbean Regional Economic Conference, p. 4.

38. Ibid, p. 17.

39. Antrobus and Peacocke. We can annihilate ourselves or we can change our ideas: two networks reflecting Third World feminist critique on the degradation of the environment and the dominant economic paradigm.

40. Antrobus. Strategies for Change: design of programmes and plans.

41. Ibid, p. 7.

42. Wilson-Henry. The poor are not powerless, p. 11.

BIBLIOGRAPHY

Andaiye: [Statement] In 'Strangers and sisters: women, race and immigration; voices from the conference "Black women speak out and claim our rights", London, England, 13 November, 1982' / edited by Selma James, - Bristol: Falling Wall Press, 1985

Antrobus, Peggy: Gender implications of the development crisis. In 'Development in suspense: selected papers and proceedings of the first conference of Caribbean Economist.' / edited by Norman Girvan and George Beckford. - Kingston: Frederich Ebert Siftung and Association of Caribbean Economists, 1989.

Antrobus, Peggy: Strategies for change: design of programmes and plans - In 'WAND Occasional Paper', 3/90, Pinelands: WAND, 1990

Antrobus, Peggy: We can annihilate ourselves or we can change our ideas: two networks reflecting Third World feminist critique on the degradation of the environment and the dominant economic paradigm / by Peggy Antrobus and Nan Peacocke. - In 'UNESCO Courier'

Baksh-Soodeen, Rawwida [Preface] by Rawwida Baksh-Soodeen and Rhoda Reddock. In 'Creation Fire: a CAFRA anthology of Caribbean Women's poetry.' / edited by Ramabai Espinet. - Toronto: Sister Vision, 1990.

Beneria, Lourdes: The crossroads of class and gender: industrial homework, subcontracting and household dynamics in Mexico City / by Lourdes Beneria and Martha Roldan. - Chicago: The University of Chicago, 1987.

CAFRA: Women in Caribbean Agriculture Research/Action Project. Overall report and summary of main findings. - Tunapuna: CAFRA, 1988.

Caribbean Community Secretariat: Study to monitor the legal status of women in member states of the Caribbean Community.- Guyana: Caribbean Community Secretariat, 1986.

Caribbean Community Secretariat: Women in Guyana: facts and figures / prepared by the University of Guyana Women's Studies Groups [et al]. - Guyana: Caribbean Community Secretariat, 1988.

Cuales, Sonia: Some theoretical considerations on social class, class consciousness and gender consciousness. In 'Gender in Caribbean Development.' / edited by Patricia Mohammed and Cathy Shepherd. - St. Augustine: UWI Women and Development Studies Project, 1988.

Cuales, Sonia: Women traders in agricultural products / prepared by Sonia Cuales and Monique Lagro.- Port of Spain, ECLAC, 1987.

Dalla Costa, Mariarosa: The power of women and the subversion of the community / by Mariarosa Dalla Costa and Selma James. - 3rd ed. Bristol: Falling Wall Press, 1975.

Danns, George K.: Domestic violence and marital relationships in the Caribbean: a Guyana case study / George K. Danns and Basmat Shiw Parsad. - Turkeyen: University of Guyana, Women Studies Unit, 1989.

Deere, Carmen: In the shadows of the sun: Caribbean development alternatives and U.S. policy / by Carmen Deere (Coordinator), Peggy Antrobus [et al], - San Francisco: Westview Press, 1990.

Drayton, Kathleen: The gender bias in education. - In 'WAND Occasional Paper', 2/91. Pinelands, WAND, 1991.

Drayton, Kathleen: Women's organisations in Barbados and regional integration. - Cave Hill: UWI, Women and Development Studies Programme, 1991.

ECLAC: Comparative status of women in selected Caribbean countries as indicated by selected social, economic, demographic and legal parameters. - Port of Spain: ECLAC, 1989.

French, Joan: Hope and disillusion: the CBI in Jamaica: a case study. Kingston: ADA, 1990.

Grenada. Department of Women's Affairs: Report on national symposium on the status of women in Grenada, Carriacou and Petite Martinique. - Grenada: Department of Women's Affairs, 1991.

The Hastings (Barbados) Statement of Women. - In 'Report of the Women and Development Unit, 10th Anniversary Consultation and Symposium' held at Caribbee Hotel, Hastings, Barbados, 7-11 November, 1988. Pinelands: WAND, 1988

Henry-Wilson, Maxine: The poor are not powerless. In 'WAND Occasional Paper' 1/91. Pinelands: WAND, 1991.

Ingram-Roberts, Audrey: The changing role of women's bureaux in the process of social change in the Caribbean / keynote presentation for the 10th Anniversary Celebrations of the Women's Affairs Unit, Ministry of Youth, Sports and Community Affairs, Nassau, Bahamas, 27 June, 1991. - Nassau: Women's Affairs Unit, 1991.

Jamaica. Bureau of Women's Affairs: The National Policy Statement on Women: the ten immediate policy goals and basic statistics. - Kingston: Bureau of Women's Affairs.

Lagro, Monique: Women Traders in St. Vincent and the Grenadines. - Port of Spain: ECLAC, 1988.

Maharaj, Niala: Fly-by-night female traders of the Caribbean islands: do they hold the key to regional integration? In 'Women in Action' 2/88.

Massiah, Joycelin: Making the invisible visible: indicators for planning for women in Caribbean development.- Cave Hill: ISER, 1989.

McAfee, Kathy: Storm signals: structural adjustment and development alternatives in the Caribbean. - London: Zed Books, 1991.

Phillips, Daphne: Women traders in Trinidad and Tobago.- Port of Spain: ECLAC, 1985.

The Port of Spain Consensus of the Caribbean Regional Economic Conference, Trinidad & Tobago, 27 February - 1 March 1991. - Port of Spain: CARICOM, 1991.

Reddock, Rhoda: The Caribbean feminist tradition - In 'Women Speak!', Nos. 26 & 27. Pinelands: WAND, 1990.

Sen, Gita: Development, crisis and alternative visions:Third World women's perspective / by Gita Sen and Caren Grown - New York: Monthly Review Press, 1987.

United Nations:The Nairobi forward-looking strategies for the advancement of women.- New York: United Nations Department of Public Information, 1986.

WAND:The involvement of Caribbean media in the implementation of the Nairobi forward-looking strategies for the advancement of women / Report of a study commissioned by UNESCO. - Pinelands: WAND, 1990.

Wiltshire, Rosina: Caribbean regional and international migration: transnational dimensions / by Rosina Wiltshire and Linda Basch. In 'Caribbean regional and international migration.' Ottawa: IDRC, 1991.

Witter, Michael:The informal economy in Jamaica: some empirical exercises. - Mona: ISER, 1990.

Women in the Caribbean - Parts 1 & 2 / edited by Joycelin Massiah. In 'Social and Economic Studies' Special Numbers, Vol. 35, No. 2, June 1986/No.3, September 1986.

APPENDIX

PARTICIPANTS IN THE APRIL 25, 1991 BRAINSTORMING SESSION

Magda Pollard, Women's Affairs Officer, CARICOM Secretariat

Olney Daly-Hill, CARICOM Secretariat

Sybil Patterson, Coordinator, Women and Development Studies, University of Guyana

Hermione McKenzie, Coordinator, Women and Development Studies, UWI, Mona

Rawwida Baksh-Soodeen, Coordinator, CAFRA

Dr. Joycelin Massiah, Director, ISER, UWI

Joan French, Coordinator, Caribbean Policy Development Centre

Dr. Christine Barrow, Consultant

Kathleen Drayton, Coordinator, Women and Development Studies Groups, Cave Hill

Dr. Rosina Wiltshire, Consultant

Dr. Patricia Ellis, Consultant

Peggy Antrobus, Tutor/Coordinator, Women and Development Unit, UWI

Jeanette Bell, Programme Coordinator, Women and Development Unit, UWI

Sheila Stuart, Coordinator, Media Productions, Women and Development Unit, UWI

Andaiye, Consultant, Women and Development Unit, UWI

Atherton Martin (left) and Reginald Rolle of Dominica (right) conversing at NGO SIDS Forum, Barbados, 1994

Globalisation, democratic deficit and civil society in the Greater Caribbean integration processes

Andrés Serbin

Venezuelan Andrés Serbin is a political scientist attached to the National System of Research of the National Council of Scientific and Technological Research as a category three researcher. He is also special Advisor on Caribbean Affairs to the Latin American Economic System (SELA) and the president of the board of directors of the Regional Centre for Social and Economic Research (CRIES). Andrés, who has been the recipient of several awards and grants for academic and professional excellence is a well-published editor and author in social and political issues.

1. GLOBALISATION AND ITS CONTRADICTIONS

The globalisation process of the contemporary world has given rise to a growing interdependence, interconnection and interrelation of the states and peoples of the planet. At the margin of its identification with a determined phase in the expansion of capitalism, in the framework of a specific cycle of the same (Wallerstein, 1995); beyond the association between the world expansion of capitalism as a hegemonic economic system and the nation-state as the dominant political model in a determined stage of Western modernity (Giddens, 1993); independently of its greater or lesser contemporary intensity and condensation (Camillieri, 1995), the fact is that we are confronting a process which affects, in an irreversible and complex way, the whole planet and which at the same time is not limited to its economic dimensions.

Currently, beyond the distinctive economic processes which characterise globalisation - intensification and liberalisation of international trade, financial globalisation and productive restructuring, techno-scientific revolution - a series of geopolitical, political, communicational, cultural and social aspects also articulate the growing inter-linking between states, nations, ethnic groups, social groups and individuals at a world level. Thus today we not only speak of the global village which McLuhan referred to several decades ago but also of global politics, global communications, global consumer habits, global issues or themes, global governance[1] and of their deleterious effects, as well as of the different ways of reacting to the same, through varied particularisms (ethnic, national, religious) or complementary or antagonistic modalities of regionalisation.

In any case, despite the uniform and basically homogenizing versions of globalisation or the references to the end of ideology or history, globalisation is seen as a multidimensional, complex and contradictory phenomenon which characterises a phase of accelerated transition in human society, and which requires a special conceptual and analytical effort for its comprehension.

It is precisely the contradictory nature of globalisation which we highlight in this article, because despite its 'homogenizing vocation' in the economic, political and cultural aspects, it engenders phenomena which are not only fragmentary but also contradictory and eventually antagonistic to its own evolution.

In fact, this phase of the world development of capitalism is formed, progressively, on the dynamics that articulate three components - the market as a growing regulating directive of the dynamics of the world economy; the nation-state as the protagonist of an international system characterised by anarchy (independently of the current reformulations and redimensionings) from the realist perspective; and the appearance of a transnational civil society, identified with the emergence, development and growing influence of a set of social actors with new and, more specifically, transnational characteristics.

It must be said that in the framework of the dynamics between market, state and civil society at a global level, the frontiers between the international and the domestic are becoming increasingly tenuous and diffuse, because commercial and financial globalisation is associated with the notable prominence of the transnational corporations and the banks and financial organisations which go beyond the territorial limits of the nation-states and exercise a decisive pressure on the formulation and implementation of their policies, both domestically and at the level of their external policies.[2]

However, at the same time, the nation-states, questioned by this process both in their external sovereignty and in their domestic undertakings, are adapting themselves progressively to this dynamic through the establishment of new regulations, international organisations and various systems in an attempt to bring under control the financial, commercial and productive factors with which they interact. Despite this, these processes increasingly question the sovereignty of the nation-states as it emerged and has been developed since the middle of the 17th century and they systematically restrict its efficiency and capacity to govern and its legitimisation in the domestic sphere, without diluting the persistence of its crucial role in the international system and in the formulation and implementation of public policies.[3]

In this framework, however, a multitude of social networks and actors of a transnational nature begin to go beyond the social and political action within the margins of the states to acquire, in turn, a protagonistic importance in the global dynamics and eventually to influence the public policies themselves. In this respect, it is enough to mention the activities of Amnesty International, Greenpeace or the women's movements to illustrate the point.

Independently of the increasingly interactive nature of these three components - market, state and civil society in the global dynamic, the appearance and recent development of the social networks and actors also question and limit, on the one hand, the traditional role of the states as key actors in the international system and, on the other, attempt to influence, regulate or modify, through the mobilisation and influence of public opinion, many of the decisions and policies which emanate from the eventual articulation of interests between the states and the transnational corporations, the multilateral economic organisations and the intergovernmental organisations. As a result, the so-called international system or global society becomes more complex because of a multiplication not only of actors but also of spheres, levels and circuits of interaction, giving rise to an extremely complex, multidimensional dynamic (Tomassini, 1993), and to the growing transnational performance of actors that Rosenau qualifies as sovereignty-free actors, in the context of a multicentral dynamic of the international system (Rosenau, 1990).

In this context, and given the contradictory nature of the process, it is not by chance that some analysts point out, on the one hand, that vis-à-vis the 'globalisation from above' promoted by states and corporations, a 'globalisation from below' (Brecher, Brown and Cutler, 1993) is developing, driven by the emerging social actors and formed on the basis of a transnational civil society and, on the other, that the eminently structural interpretations of the world system in formation do not take into account the relevant role which these new actors and their different and fragmented projects of contra-hegemony are beginning to acquire (Cox, 1987).

These approaches, however, require special fine-tunings, in particular with reference to the theoretical and conceptual scope of the term 'global civil society'.

2. THE SOCIALISATION OF GLOBALISATION AND GLOBAL CIVIL SOCIETY

In the last twenty years, a proliferation of non-state networks and actors has emerged on the international scene, including a broad spectrum of humanitarian, religious or labour organisations; social movements of different kinds, or organisations that promote specific global issues in the areas of peace, human rights, development and ecological balance (Coate, Alger, Lipechutz, 1996, 103). Many have emerged as a result of their links and relations with intergovernmental organisations (IGOs) and, especially, with the agencies of the United Nations Organisation (UN) and, in particular, with its Economic and Social Council (ECOSOC); others have emerged and have been developed around specific issues and grievances of a global or regional nature, based on the emergence of fora in the framework of the Rio Ecological Summit, the Stockholm Social Summit or the activities promoted by the International Women's Year; finally, some others respond to their own dynamics and issues as in the already mentioned cases of Amnesty International, Greenpeace or Oxfam. Together with these expressions more specifically associated with the globalisation process, as a reaction to this, varied forms of particularisms with a growing global and transnational nature have also been developed, either of an ethnic, national or religious nature, which question the globalisation process and especially the expressions of western modernity associated with it (Badie-Smouts, 1992).

Some of these actors and organisations respond to the characterisation of non-governmental organisations of different types; others to social movements with different characteristics; but, taken as a whole, they respond to a vision of politics which exceeds the exclusive reference of the national or the nation state, which gives rise to a global perspective and postulates new modalities for approaching politics at a planetary level.

In principle, when it is a question of NGOs, their defining characteristics refer to their character as formal organisations, with institutional continuity; which aspire to govern themselves on the basis of constitutional arrangements or their own rules for functioning; they are private in the sense of being autonomous with respect to the governments and they do not have the capacity to lead or direct in the respective societies; they link organisations from several countries; they promote a variety of social issues; they are non-profit-making or do not seek pecuniary benefits; and basically they have transnational objectives, operations and connections (Gordenker/Weiss, 1995, 20).

The majority maintain a variety of links with governments and other non-governmental organisations but predominantly, as a whole, they frequently seek to limit the action of the states and, eventually, of the market, especially their most prominent actors - the transnational corporations and the financial organisations, both private and intergovernmental. In this respect, they tend to promote their activities beyond 'the conventional categories of the state and enterprise' (ibid. 19) and, essentially, they tend to politicise previously non-politicised spheres and to connect the local with the global, linking their activities to locally-based grass-root organisations, national and international non-governmental organisations (Macdonald, 1994, 277).[4]

On the other hand, globalisation has also given rise to the development of 'new social movements' of a transnational nature, understood as 'a collective actor made up of individuals which understand they have common interests and, at least as far as a significant part of their social existence is concerned, a common identity' (Scott, 1990, 6). To promote these interests, they have the capacity of mass mobilisation or use this capacity as an element of pressure and which distinguishes them from other collective actors such as political parties, pressure groups or voluntary associations. In particular, what differentiates them from these associations and some NGOs is their concern about defending or changing existing society, or the search to change the relative position of the group they represent in society.

The difference between the old and new social movements does not consist so much of the greater scope of the transnational projection of the latter in the framework of globalisation; while the former tend to organise themselves around divisions of a class nature (labour movement, peasant movements), the second articulate themselves around social contradictions such as gender, lifestyles, the environment, racial inequality and war (Straw, 1994, 651), so that they expand the notion of the political to a much broader sphere which includes the social and the cultural.

In essence, this complex and contradictory mesh of different social organisations and actors, articulated via the transnational networks, with global interests and grievances and frequently with roots in local interests and grievances, gives rise to the appearance of a global civil society which 'reproduces in its interactions the conflicts and contradictions of the domestic civil societies from which they emerge and, at the same time, create new ones which reflect the dynamic of power at an international level' (Macdonald, 1994, 285). But at the same time, it expresses not only the impact of economic globalisation in general terms, but it also corresponds to the globalisation of state power in a mottled and complex addition of national state power to global power which characterises the current inter-state system, with its accelerated transitional change and its contradictions (Straw, 1994, 650).

In any case, both the different expressions of non-governmental organisations and the different social movements of a transnational nature have given rise to a global civil society, defined by its own codes and legal rules, frequently in opposition to and autonomous from the states, through the creation and development of transnational networks which generate new political spaces in the international system. However, as Lipechutz points out (1992), this process in turn has given rise to a questioning of the dominant central-state discourse which is manifested both through the emergence of this global civil society, and through the different ethnic, religious and nationalist particularisms, questioning the very ideology of globalisation.

In this respect, these actors in their heterogeneity tend to promote governance in spheres and areas of the international system, beyond, or in association with the governments' action, because they develop 'the capacity of getting things done without the legal power to order them to be done' (Czempiel, 1992, 250). From this perspective, and in the framework of the pointing out that while 'there is no world government, there is global governance', together with the institutionalised regulatory arrangements in the different partial systems at a global level, less formalised rules, regulations and procedures are developed and enforced which impose patterns on international conduct without having recourse to written constitutions or material power (Coate, Algier, Lipechutz, 1996, 99), questioning the realist vision of an anarchic international system.

In this process, the role of the different emerging social actors at a transnational level becomes increasingly crucial and gives rise to the appearance of a global civil society which generates, in the words of Camillieri (1995, 218), a blurring of social control by eroding the power of the states and which postulates a civil society that, unlike the domestic one, has as a reference not the state but the different forms of inter-state and international articulation of power.

However, it is necessary to understand that civil society in general and emerging global civil society in particular do not constitute a homogeneous and unified actor. In fact, global civil society, apart from constituting a response to globalisation in terms of a 'globalisation from below' and of trying, along general lines, to limit and influence the states' action by introducing forms of global governance, is also marked by contradictions and conflicts (Macdonald, 1994, 269). In the Gramscian acceptance of the term, civil society is a field of conflict between hegemonic and counter-hegemonic forces, but in the case of global civil society, this picture is complicated further because it reproduces the conflicts and contradictions of the domestic civil societies from which it emerges, at the same time creating new contradictions which reflect the dynamics of power at an international level and the same role of the market and the state. This complication also reveals itself in several ways.

Secondly, the traditional notion of civil society refers to different non-state actors which include formal representative organisations such as political parties, churches, labour unions and professional associations; formal organisations of a functional kind (schools, universities and the mass media), and more informal political and social networks (which range from local voluntary groups and ad hoc coalitions of activists to coordinated social movements at a national or international level) (Straw, 1994, 648). In this perspective, global civil society is formed not only by the NGOs (recognised by the IGOs and by the governments as regards global issues), by social movements based on class of an international nature that precede the current emergence of global civil society (such as peasant and labour movements or the political internationals of the left) or by the formal mechanisms of socialisation which are expanding at a transnational level, but also by a series of 'new social movements' with an international projection which frequently go beyond the traditional notions of politics and citisenship, by articulating cultural approaches linked to specific values and lifestyles.

So that the traditional notions of a civil society divided horizontally on the basis of hegemonic and counter-hegemonic projects, in the framework of global civil society (and frequently on the basis of accelerated changes in the domestic civil societies), are complicated by the presence of different forms of vertical articulation not only around grievances and projects of a global nature promoted by different NGOs but also on the basis of less institutionalised initiatives of different social movements with a cultural emphasis[5]. Incidentally, we must add to this picture of vertical divisions the different ways these actors use the influence of public opinion and the mass media which are frequently crucial instruments, together with national and international mobilisation to exercise pressure on governments and also on intergovernmental organisations or to question governmental projects.

Thirdly, an element to be considered is that together with the internal divisions and contradictions of global civil society introduced by the different modalities of relating to the established institutions of power or financial and productive control, and the different forms of political and political-cultural expression of the transnational social actors, a fundamental division is that which establishes, in a frequently ambiguous and diffuse way, a division between the transnational social actors of the North and those of the South. In this respect, while post-Cold War events have significantly blurred the traditional dichotomy between North and South (because the concentration of commercial, financial and technological dynamics has been increasingly in the three political-economic focal points of Europe, North America and Japan, and the political-economic similarities and convergences of the South have tended to differentiate, fragment and dilute the very notion of a homogeneous developing South to the extent of proposing that 'the third world is dead' - Olsen, 1995) this persists manifestly in the relations between the social actors of the North and South. The same category of DONGOs implies, in essence, a vertical relation between the NGOs of the North and the South, because the former frequently dictate or influence, through the allocation of resources for programmes, the agendas of the latter in the framework of the transnational networks which link both.

On the other hand, the same linking of the respective NGOs (particularly in the case of the GONGOs or QUANGOs) with the respective states of the North conditions circumstantially their strategies and agendas, especially as regards ecological, human rights and peace and security issues, vis-à-vis the promotion of nationalist positions of the states in the South which, at the same time and in a distinctive way, eventually conditions the performance - cooperative, reactive or antagonistic - of the NGOs or social movements in the South, especially as regards socio-political and economic issues like development, inequality, poverty and unemployment. In short, despite the frequently autonomous nature of many of these social actors with respect to the respective states, their socio-political base is reflected not only in the actions of the same but also influences the actions of many NGOs and social movements.

In conclusion, and given these traits, despite the relevant characteristics which a global civil society acquires in the emerging international system under the impact of the globalisation process, in interlocution and interaction, whether critical or otherwise, with the state and the market, it is evident that this civil society is not free of the complexities and contradictions introduced by globalisation.

In this framework, one of the question marks is nevertheless how, with the emergence of a global civil society as a relevant factor in the international dynamic, it can influence the process concomitant to globalisation, overcoming the 'democratic deficit' engendered by the deployment of 'globalitarian' alternatives where states, intergovernmental organisations and transnational economic agents take decisions without the participation or control of broad social sectors of the planet which, however, are decisively affected by these decisions. While this is a very broad question mark, it affects, on the level of specific policies, the evolution of the globalisation process because it questions the orientation of 'globalisation from above' by proposing a globalisation with the increasing participation not only of countries and regions at the margin of the international economic system but also of specific social sectors and actors in the emerging global civil society. This question mark is particularly relevant in the sphere of the regionalisation processes which, as a response and complement to globalisation, are developing in Latin America and the Caribbean.

3. REGIONALISATION AND DEMOCRATIC DEFICIT IN THE INTEGRATION PROCESSES IN LATIN AMERICA AND THE CARIBBEAN

Given the threat of exclusion or marginalisation from the international economic system as a result of the globalisation process, the Latin American and Caribbean countries have reacted, since the end of the 1980s, by reactivating, deepening or developing regional and sub-regional integration processes, in a broad spectrum which includes the reactivation of the Central American Common Market (MCCA) through the creation of the SIECA, CARICOM and the Andean Group to the creation of MERCOSUR, the Group of Three (G-3) and the Association of Caribbean States (ACS) (Serbin, 1995; 1996). Independently of the scope that of each of these schemes attempts to achieve with regard to integration - ranging from free trade agreements like the G-3 to regional political platforms like the ACS via different varieties of common market and customs unions, a common denominator has been their identification with the hypotheses of open regionalism promoted by the ECLAC.

In this respect, together with the explicit objective of promoting, in the framework of the adjustment policies predominating in the countries in the region under the effects of the 'Washington consensus' and the neo-liberal approaches of the multilateral financial organisations, a more active intra-regional commercial exchange and a competitive insertion in the world economy, the new forms of regionalism in Latin America and the Caribbean have been associated with the attempt to link these initiatives more closely with the government and entrepreneurial sectors in the framework of the adjustment programmes under way. In fact, generally it has meant a growing conjunction between the Latin American and Caribbean political and economic elite in the initiatives aimed at going deeper into regionalisation, frequently evident in the way governments consult the entrepreneurial sector in the free trade and integration processes through the 'next room' modality in regional negotiations, or in the establishment of formal consultation mechanisms with this sector through the Consultation Councils created in the Andean Group, MERCOSUR, the Central American integration system or CARICOM.

However, in these processes, the absence of participation of the other actors in civil society - both the social movements and even, with shades and variations, formal political actors like the political parties - has been repeatedly made evident. With the exception of the participation, in some of the schemes, of the labour sector through consultation mechanisms or tripartite mechanisms with the participation of the government and businessmen, the remaining social actors have not been represented most of the regionalisation processes. In practice, the dominant tendency in the incorporation of social actors, where this occurs, in Latin America and the Caribbean has been through tripartism, on the basis of integrating, in a consultative capacity, the entrepreneurial sector and the labour sector, through their union representatives, together with government representatives, in consultation mechanisms. A clear illustration in this respect is linked with the Working Subgroup No. 11 of Labour Relations, Employment and Social Security of MERCOSUR and the proposed Economic and Social Consultation Forum (FCES) of the same scheme, with consultative and advisory faculties, but not the capacity to adopt decisions. As one analyst points out, however, the FCES 'is still waiting for a greater definition' and does not include other social actors (Podesta, 1995a and b). Likewise, the inclusion of non-governmental socio-economic actors in this type of consultation mechanism, despite the early appearance of the social issue in the integration process, generally comes after its creation and advances, even as regards the labour sector (ibidem).

In a similar way, in the Andean Group, while the social question received significant attention and gave rise to the creation of the Business Consultation Council and the Labour Consultation Council, the Andean Social Charter approved by the Andean Parliament also responds to a tripartist conception, taking into account the government, business and labour sectors, but with a limited reference to other groups basically represented by women, children and the family (Fundación Freiderich Ebert-PRS, 1994, 57).

In this respect, the role that the labour union traditions play and the importance of these organisations in the Latin American context is evident, added to the growing concern about the proposals of "social dumping" in the GATT and the WTO, and the effects of globalisation and productive restructuring on the labour markets and employment.

Paradoxically, since the 1980s numerous social movements and non-governmental organisations have burst onto the domestic scene in most Latin American and Caribbean countries, especially with reference to issues like human rights, defence of the environment, gender rights and indigenous grievances and rights. At the same time, many of them have acquired a transnational projection, both at a regional and global level, as in the case of the women's, human rights and indigenous movements, giving rise to the development of a social network which eventually forms the germ of a regional civil society, despite the cleavages and divisions engendered by different sub-regional political and cultural experiences - between the Andean societies and the Southern Cone societies; the Central American and Caribbean societies; the Amazon conglomerate and the Caribbean Basin processes.

However, these actors and civil society in general, frequently impacted not only by the adjustment programmes but also by the direct or indirect effects of the regional agreements, have been absent from a participation in the decision-making in these processes and from any influence on the course of these initiatives, in the framework of the maxim 'we shall decide on your behalf, for you, but without you'.

This significant 'democratic deficit' in the implementation of the regionalisation processes occurs in a context where, in an increasingly notable way, civil society claims a greater participation and demands a degree of accountability of the respective governments in a decision-making process with which it has nothing whatsoever to do despite its devastating social effects in terms of the growth in inequality and social polarisation, poverty and unemployment in the societies in the region.

Despite the recognition since the last decade by the United Nations agencies and organisations of the need to link, consult and eventually implement joint programmes with the NGOs and social movements or the limited attempts by the European Union to overcome this 'deficit', both the governments and the regional intergovernmental organisations in Latin America and the Caribbean have tended to react with reticence to the demands and proposals of the regional social actors, and have generally avoided a deepening of the implementation of mechanisms for their participation or consultation.

In this respect, while the formal political actors - parties and labour unions - have found channels of expression through the regional Parliaments, in the first case, or consultation mechanisms (including specific aspects such as the proposal of a social charter in the Andean Group), in the second case, assuming the socio-political components of their participation, the remaining actors in civil society (with the exception of the business groups and unions) have been excluded from this process, despite the appearance and progressive consolidation of the network of a society or a set of regional civil societies in Latin America and the Caribbean.

In this framework, the trilogy of the regional articulation of state, market and civil society, shows evidence of a significant weakening of the recognition and institutionalisation of the participation or political interlocution of the latter, similar to the one mentioned in the general framework of the globalisation process.

However, the mobilisation of the actors in the regional civil society - movements of women and ecologists, indigenous organisation and human rights in particular - has had an impact with their claims not only on public opinion and the mass media but it has also begun to exercise a growing influence on the states and, eventually, on the corporations and financial organisations.

4. CIVIL SOCIETY AND DEMOCRATIC PARTICIPATION IN THE REGIONALISATION PROCESS IN THE GREATER CARIBBEAN

The globalisation process and the regionalising reactions, and also the conceptions associated with open regionalism and the Washington consensus, with the differences in each case, have also significantly affected all the societies in the Greater Caribbean[6] which are mostly demographically and territorially small, economically vulnerable and geopolitically sensitive. The region by itself, beyond its original geopolitical differentiation in the framework of the Cold War, presents an extensive cultural and ethnic as well as political heterogeneity, as a consequence of the different legacies and traditions of the different colonial systems which were established there.

The recent creation of the ACS, however, validates a new conception of the region, in the framework of the globalisation process underway, which permits, on the basis of political coincidences, the search for economic cooperation and the emergence of a regional 'social community' with its own characteristics, the overcoming of differences and of heterogeneity on the basis of common values and the defence of the Caribbean Sea and the societies which live there (Association of Caribbean States, 1994).

However, the act of constitution of the ACS itself presents a series of limitations as regards the participation of different social actors in the regionalisation and integration process, particularly in its reference to the recognised social actors and their participation mechanisms in the decision-making process.

Together with the different references to 'social partners' or 'social actors' in the document and the rules of recognition and formal acknowledgement of them in the ACS, with different conceptions about the same and their role in the regionalisation process, there are marked differences in the experiences, histories and political cultures of the different sub-regions which lead to different conceptions and emphasis in their treatment by the governments. In this respect, the political cultures and traditions of the Greater Caribbean include a very broad range of historical experiences with particular effects on the conceptions about the participation of civil society and democratic governance which in turn is reflected in the attitudes and perceptions of the governments and their representatives vis-à-vis the participation of an emerging regional civil society in the integration process. In fact, the political history of the member countries of the Group of Three, the Central American countries, Cuba and the Dominican Republic, Haiti and Suriname, and of the English-speaking countries in the Caribbean mark the outlines of a complex political heterogeneity and different attitudes and perceptions vis-à-vis the participation of civil society in the governance process in general and of regional integration in particular.

To take only two of the most important sub-regions - the English-speaking Caribbean and the Central American sub-region - their different recent political histories lead to marked differences in the traditions and conceptions of political participation in civil society in the regionalisation process. In the case of Central America it must be noted, in the first place, that together with the Central American Parliament created as a consultation forum for the representatives of political parties in the area and despite a broad consultation made between 1972 and 1976 with the social actors on the part of the High Level Committee for the Restructuring and Improvement of the Central American Common Market (CAN), the resulting project was not accepted by the governments of the region in the framework of the crisis affecting Central America (de la Ossa, 1996, 20). However, once the pacification process begun with the Esquipulas agreements was underway and the Central American integration process was reactivated with the creation of the Central American Integration System (SICA) in 1991, the Tegucigalpa protocol which gave rise to it established the constitution of a Central American Consultation Council, formed by 'the business, labour and academic sectors and the other main active forces in the Central American Isthmus representing the economic, social and cultural sectors, committed to the effort of isthmic integration' (ibidem, 21).

Despite this initiative, on the one hand, a series of criticisms emerged because of the 'unilateral selective criteria' used by the Secretariat General of SICA to establish an earlier group in order to organise it and prepare its basic rules (ibidem) and, on the other hand, divergences between the organisations of civil society as regards the representation on the Committee, especially between the Central American Intersectorial Coordination Committee (CACI), created in 1993, and the Civil Initiative for Central American Integration (ICIC), constituted in April 1994 (Vargas Roldon, 1996, 7).[7]

However, despite these initial difficulties, on 2 November 1995 the Consultation Committee of the Central American Integration System (SS-SICA) was established as 'initially a consultation entity for the regionally organised civil society, with the object of institutionalizing the participation of the economic and social actors in the decision-making process within Central American integration', with the participation of 17 regional organisations, including FEDEPRICAP representing the business chambers; CTCA, CCT and COCENTRA as the three main groups of unionised workers in Central America; CONCAPE for the small and medium-sized enterprises; CCC-CA for the cooperatives in the region; FECAICA for the industrial entrepreneurs in the region; FECAMCO representing the chambers of commerce; FECATRINS for the transporters; ASOCODE for the organised peasants; AUPRICA and CSUCA representing the private and state universities; CONCERTACION CENTROAMERICANA which groups the non-governmental organisations; UPROCAFE representing the small and medium-sised coffee producers; the Central American chapter of the World Council of Indigenous Peoples; the Central American Council of Education and Cultural Workers; and FEMICA which groups the municipal governments in the region (Vargas Roldan, 1996, 7-8). This extensive list of organisations of a regional nature which advocates the integration of the isthmus and the participation of civil society in this process via regional mechanisms does not end with the organisations mentioned, since the regional women's organisation and the Human Rights organisations (CODEHUCA) are also in the process of incorporation (ibidem).

It is important to highlight that together with organisations from the business, labour, and cultural/academic sectors, not only the indigenous and cooperative organisations participate in the SICA Consultation Committee but also those NGOs which act in more than three countries in the region. The Consultation Committee constitutes a regional forum whose representatives are appointed by the respective organisations and not by the governments, and its decisions are taken unanimously and not by a majority.

In the case of the CARICOM countries, the decolonisation processes which bore the English-speaking Caribbean countries to independence were originally promoted by the local labour unions which frequently gave rise to, or were linked with, the political parties which led them to political independence. These origins, especially in the final stages of the Second World War, could have given rise to a tripartist vision of the participation of the political and social actors in the integration process, similar to the one pointed out in the case of MERCOSUR and perhaps with the significant difference of an early incorporation of the labour unions in the process. However, the convergence of a growing deterioration process in the unions and the traditional political parties in the sub-region under the effects of the globalising changes and the end of the cold war (Serbin, 1995), together with the existence of a tradition of non-governmental community activities has given rise to a greater projection and relevance of the importance of other actors of civil society in the CARICOM integration process (Duncan, 1996).

By way of illustration, it suffices to point out that in 1993, this organisation had proposed the creation of an Assembly of Parliaments of the Caribbean Community recently approved, while since the end of the 1980s, the West Indian Commission itself and CARICOM have postulated a Civil Society Charter for the Caribbean Community, to 'create a truly participatory political atmosphere in the heart of the Caribbean Community which may be propitious for genuine consultation in the governance process' (CARICOM, 1993).

In this framework, as a consequence of an initial participation by non-governmental organisations in the Regional Economic Conference convened by CARICOM in 1991, in 1992 the governments of the CARICOM member countries adopted the recommendation, in article XX of the Charter, that the signatory states 'take measures to establish in their respective states (territories) a framework for continuous and genuine consultation which involves the social partners consisting of political parties, the business community, labour unions, non-governmental organisations, disadvantaged social groups and other bodies representative of the community's interests in order to achieve common agreements and support for the objectives, contents and implementation of the national and social programmes' (pages 16-17).

In this perspective the Caribbean Policy Development Centre (CPDC), based in Barbados and established by non-governmental organisations in February 1991 as a regional network of NGOs, is making progress in the possibility of being recognised as a CARICOM consultation mechanism. The objective of the CPDC, which groups more than 21 English-, French-, Spanish- and Dutch-speaking organisations from the Caribbean of a regional, sub-regional or national nature with a regional perspective, aims at 'understanding where and how the policies are formulated and how they affect our daily lives; to share information about these policies; develop the confidence and ability of the Caribbean people to influence public policy, support policies that favour the Caribbean people; and work together to change policies that do not benefit the Caribbean people' (Wedderburn, 1996). This organisation groups a wide range of organisations from civil society, conceived as non-governmental organisations in a broad sense and which includes development agencies, religious organisations, groups of women and young people, people's theater workers, economists, social communicators, human rights and peasant organisations and indigenous peoples (ibidem, 8).

On the basis of alternative approaches to the regional development strategies postulated in the framework of the adjustment programmes, the CPDC has developed an important interlocution with the CARICOM with the object of obtaining recognition, together with the labour unions and the business sector, for its consultation status as the third 'social partner' in the integration process, to the extent that in July 1995, the CARICOM heads of government accepted its incorporation in the regional Consultative Council.

5. TOWARD A REGIONAL CIVIL SOCIETY? THE PROBLEMS OF CIVIL SOCIETY'S PARTICIPATION IN THE REGIONALISATION PROCESS

This superficial review of the organisation processes of civil society in two of the sub-regions in the Greater Caribbean and their current achievements as regards participation in the regionalisation process poses a series of tentative conclusions but also a series of questions.

In the first place, it must be pointed out that the emergence of a regional civil society appears to be marked by the development of the consolidation and participation processes of the emerging civil societies at a sub-regional level - as in the case of Central American and the Caribbean, with few or limited links between them in this stage and strongly marked by the respective experiences and political legacies. In this respect, a first comparison between the two sub-regions makes it possible to point, in a preliminary and tentative way, to a greater development and a greater participation of the NGOs, including the religious ones, in the Caribbean and a more reduced presence of the same in the participation in the Central American integration process. Likewise, the development of an apparently more fluid interlocution process between the governments, CARICOM and regional civil society in the Caribbean must be mentioned, while in Central America the incorporation of civil society in the integration process has run into greater reticence on the part of the governments and because of internal contradictions.

Secondly, this incipient process of the incorporation of civil society in regionalisation, through a deepening of its own organisation and, institutionalisation indicates its growing development but still does not mark distinctive participation modalities at a regional level beyond its consultative nature in the framework of mechanisms agreed and promoted together with the intergovernmental organisations of sub-regional integration.

Thirdly, we must note the limited linking between political bodies of institutionalised representation at a sub-regional level - such as the Assembly of Caribbean Parliamentarians and the Central American Parliament (PAELACEN), and the organisations of civil society - such as the CPDC, the CAIC and the ICIC respectively, marking in principle an apparent divorce between the political parties and the initiatives of civil society. In this respect, on the one hand the frequent criticism by these organisations of the traditional political parties must be highlighted and, on the other hand, their insistence on the need to go beyond representative democracy towards a participatory democracy. These proposals on a political level are frequently articulated with criticisms of the development strategies promoted by the governments and proposals of alternative strategies which give more emphasis to social demands and the needs of social sectors marginalised in poverty and unemployment at a sub-regional level.

However, it is important to highlight, in the fourth place, the growing presence being acquired by a network of social actors at a regional level, with the forming (in the framework of the regionalisation processes) of a regional civil society which promotes a series of initiatives in the direction of a 'regionalisation from below' that takes into account the demands and needs of broad sectors of the population affected both by the consequences of the globalisation process and the impact of the measures which accompany the deepening of regionalisation.

Finally, on the regional and hemispheric level, these preliminary conclusions pose a series of specific questions.

In the first place, up to what point can the development of these sub-regional experiences be channelled, overcoming language, ethnic and historical barriers, toward the formation of a civil regional society in the Greater Caribbean? And secondly, up to what point can the political and social differences and heterogeneities outlined give rise to common positions as regards the definition of mechanisms of participation in the regionalisation process of the Greater Caribbean and, in particular, in the framework of the Association of Caribbean States? In this same respect, a third question arises about this intergovernmental organisation's capacity to promote and design suitable mechanisms to promote this participation in the context of the political heterogeneities and dissimilarities which characterise the region.

Lastly, on the hemispheric level, it is worth asking if these experiences are applicable to the other integration processes in Latin America, with its different political cultures and traditions and its own pace of progress in integration, in the sense that a regional civil society may emerge and that a broader participation of the same may be promoted in the integration process in Latin America and the Caribbean.

The opinions expressed in this article are personal and do not compromise any of the institutions mentioned.

BIBLIOGRAPHY

Asociación de Estados del Caribe (1994) Carta Constitutiva.

Badie, Batrand et Marie-Claude Smouts (1992) Le retournement du monde [Le Retournement du Monde], Paris: Presses de la Fondation National des Sciences Politiques et Dalloz.

Brecher, Jeremy; John Brown Childs, and Jill Cutler (1993) Global Visions. Beyond the New World Order, Boston: South End Press.

Camillieri, Joseph A. (1995) "State, Civil Society and Economy", in Camilleri, Joseph; Anthony P. Jarvis and Albert J. Paolini eds. The State in Transition. Reimagining Political Space, Boulder: Lynne Rienner.

CARICOM (1993) Charter of Civil Society for CARICOM, Georgetown, June 1993.

Coate, Roger; Chadwick F. Alger and Ronnie Lipschutz (1996) "The United Nations and Civil Society: Creative Partnership for Sustainable Development", in Alternatives, vol. 21, No. 1, Jan-Mar., pp. 93-122.

Cox, Robert W. (1987) Production, Power and World Order. Social Forces in the Making of History, New York: Columbia University Press.

Czempiel, Ernst-Otto (1992) "Governance and democratisation", in Rosenau, James N. and Ernst-Otto Czempiel (eds.) Governance without government: order and change in world politics, Cambridge: Cambridge University Press, pp. 250-270.

De la Ossa, Alvaro (1996) "Cuenca del Caribe: Mecanismos para profundizar la participación de 109 actores sociales en el proceso de regionalización", paper presented to conference on "La nueva agenda sociopolítica del proceso de integración en el Gran Caribe", February 12 & 13, 1996, INVESP/SEI A, Caracas.

Duncan, Neville (1996) "A New model of Governance and Community Development", paper presented to regional workshop on "Actores politicos e integración regional en el Gran Caribe", May 2 &3, 1996, INVESP/IRIPAZ/SELA, Guatemala.

Fundación Friederich Ebert/Proyecto Regional Sindical (1995) La carte social andina, Caracas.

Giddens, A (1993) Consecuencias de 1a modernidad, Madrid: Alianza Universidad.

Gordenker, Leon and Thomas G. Weiss (1995) "Pluralising Global Governance: Analytical Approaches and Dimensions", in Thomas G. Weiss and Leon Gordenker (eds.) NGOs, the UN and Global Governance, Boulder: Lynne Rienner, pp. 17-50.

Lipshutz, Ronnie (1992) "Reconstructing World Politics: The Emergence of Global Civil Society", in Millennium, vol. 21, No. 3, pp. 389-420.

Macdonald, Laura (1994) "Globalizing Civil Society: Interpreting International NGOs in Central America", in Millennium (?) vol. 23, No. 2, pp. 267-286.

Olsen, Gorm Rye (1995) "North-South relations in the Process of Change:The Significance of International Civil Society", in The European Journal of Development Research, vol. 7, No. 2, December, pp. 233-256.

Podesta, Bruno (1995a) "La representación socio-profesional en los paises del Mercosur en relación al CES", año 2, No. 6, March-April, pp. 229-235.

(1995b) "Seís comentarios sobre la cuestión social", paper prepared for the Conference "La dimensión social de la integración regional", 24-29 April, 1995, CEFIR, Santiago de Chile.

Rosenau, James N. (1990) Turbulence in World Politics. A Theory of Change and Continuity, Princeton: Princeton University Press.

Serbin, Andrés (1995) "Los desafíos del proceso de regionalización de la Cuenca del Caribe: integración, soberania, democracía e identidad", in Revista Venezolana de Economía y Ciencias Sociales, No. 4, pp. 75-112.

(1996) El ocaso de las islas, El Gran Caribe frente a los desafíos globales y regionales, Caracas: Nueva Sociedad/INVESP.

Scott, Alan (1990) Ideology and the New Social Movements; London: Routledge.

Shaw, Martin (1994) "Civil Society and Global Politics: Beyond a Social Movements Approach", in Millennium, vol. 23, No. 3, pp. 647668.

Tomassini, Luciano (1993) Estado, gobernabilidad y desarrollo, Washington: Serie de Monografias del Banco Interamericano de Desarrollo.

Vargas Roldan, Jorge (1996) "Los actores de la sociedad civil en el proceso de integración centroamericana", paper presented to workshop on "Los actores politicos y la integración en el Gran Caribe", May 2-3, 1996, INVESP/IRIPAZ/SELA, Guatemala.

Wallerstein, Immanuel (1995) After Liberalism, New York: the New Press.

Wedderburn, Judith (1996) "Organisations and Social Actors in the Regionalisation Process, paper presented to Conference on "La nueva agenda sociopolítico de la integración en el Gran Caribe", INVESP/SELA, xFebruary 12-13, Caracas.

NOTES

1. It is necessary to differentiate between the Anglo-Saxon term 'governance' and the notion of governability in Spanish, as Tomassini points out, because the latter includes the former and refers to broader processes that include authority's capacity to channel the interests of civil society, the interaction that emerges between both segments and, therefore, the legitimacy of the first of these: the government (Tomassini, 1993).
2. As Flak points out (1996, 15) 'The State is being subtly deformed as an instrument of human well-being by the dynamics of globalisation, which are pushing the state by degrees and to varying extent into a subordinate relationship with global market forces'. On the difficult interrelation between states and the dynamics of the market, and their effects on the sovereignty of the former, see Strange and Camillieri.
3. See Guehenno, 1993 and Ohmae, 1995.
4. A recent typology classifies them in specific NGOs with the characteristics referred to: GONGO (government-organised non-governmental organisations), promoted by governments especially in the framework of the Cold War; QUANGOs (quasi-non-governmental organisations) which despite maintaining a certain autonomy receive government resources like many NGOs in the Scandinavian countries and Canada; DONGOs (donor-organised NGO) differentiated by their sources of resources (ibidem, 21). In any case, in any of the categories, the NGOs do not govern nor do they attempt to govern, but they attempt to impose some measure of "accountability" on governments and enterprises and to manage complex interrelations and political, economic and social changes, promoting in some case cooperation with and between other actors, with special emphasis on governments (ib., 19).
5. As Lipschutz points out, in reality there is not one but several heteronomous transnational political networks in the framework of global civil society, because of the different "imaginary communities" proposed (Lipschutz, 1992, 391).
6. By Greater Caribbean we mean the region formed by a number of states, associated states and colonial territories in the Caribbean Sea, and includes both the insular states and territories and states which border the Caribbean - the Central American Countries, Mexico, Colombia, Venezuela, Guyana and Suriname, in accordance with the concept introduced by the creation of the Association of Caribbean States in 1994.
7. The CAI consists of the Federation of Private Enterprises of Central America and Panama (FEDEPRICAP); the Latin American Workers Union (CLAT); the Central American Workers Confederation (CCT); the Central American chapter of the World Council of Indigenous Peoples; the Central American Council of Education and Cultural Workers; the Central American Peasant Council (COCECA); the Caribbean and Central American Confederation of Cooperatives (CCC-CA); the Central American Transporters Federation; the Central American Higher University Council (CSUCA), and the Central American Association of Private Universities, while the ICIC consists of the Central American Association of Peasant Organisations for Cooperation and

Development (ASOCADE); the Caribbean and Central American Confederation of Cooperatives (CCC-CA); the Central American Workers Coordinator (COCENTRA); the Central American Confederation of Small and Medium-sised Industry (CONCAPE); the Central American Coordinator of Development Organisations (CONCERTACION CENTROAMERICANA); the Central American Workers Confederation (CTCA-ORIT); the Central American Federation of Communal Organisations (FECOP); and the Union of Small and Medium-sised Coffee Producers of Mexico, Central American and the Caribbean (UPROCAFE) (de la Osea, 1996, 38).

Caribbean participants meeting at the Social Summit, Copenhagen, Denmark, March 1995.

Democracy and governability in integration and regionalisation processes in the Wider Caribbean

Francine Jácome

Francine Jácome, currently resident in Caracas, Venezuela, was born in Quito, Ecuador. She has been director of the Venezuelan Institute of Social and Political Science since 1994 and is a doctoral student in Political Science. Francine has directed research projects for a number of al and international agencies and participated as organiser, chair and presenter on social and political issues in a number of international fora. She was chosen for the Researchers Promotion System of the National Council of Science and Technology in 1991 and received a Junior Lecture Fellowship from LASA in 1994. Ms. Jácome has published extensively in her field.

Introduction

In order to formulate proposals for a socio-political integration in the wider Caribbean it is fundamental to debate the variables of democracy and governability in the processes of integration and regionalisation. For the present we would say that there are two ways to incorporate the aforementioned variables in the discussion on integration and regionalisation. The predominant approach restricts the discussion to the fact that participation in the different schema of integration requires democratic governments to demonstrate acceptable levels of governability in their internal political systems. Thus both governability and democracy are restricted to the sphere of national political systems.

Nevertheless, as schema for integration are developed and a process of regionalisation is encouraged, it seems to be equally valid to analyse both democracy and governability in an international context. In this way, we would put forward the inclusion of issues such as democracy in the schema of integration and regional governability.

However, such a discussion merits, in the first place, a definition of what we will consider to be democracy and governability. Therefore, the first part of this discussion is intended to analyse the state of the art in regard to these two fundamental concepts for this work. Given the results of this latter analysis, in the second part, we will give a synthetic description of democracy and governability in the region, in order subsequently to make preliminary proposals around the questions of democracy and governability in the processes of integration and regionalisation in the wider Caribbean.

DEMOCRACY AND GOVERNABILITY:THE CURRENT DEBATE

DEMOCRACY

Currently what persists is what has traditionally been the fundamental point in the debate on democracy: how to define it. Thus, Diamond (1996) has demonstrated that confusion continues and meanings abound in relation to the concept. Notwithstanding this confusion and diversity of concepts, he indicates that there seems to be consensus around the idea that democracy is a system of political authority, separate from economic and social factors (Diamond: 1996, p. 21) and that the basic differences gravitate around the dimensions of the political attributes which encompass democracy.

In this way he proposes that there are currently two basic concepts of democracy: electoral democracy and liberal democracy. The former, put forward following a definition by Joseph Schumpeter and expanded by authors such as Samuel Huntington and Robert Dahl, gives priority to the role of elections in the definition of a democratic system: a democracy exists insofar as elections take place. Clearly, however, as Diamond argues, periodic elections can take place without this necessarily meaning that a given political system is democratic.

In contrast to this restricted definition, the concept of a liberal democracy adds many elements to that of carrying out periodic elections, in order to arrive at a definition of democracy. In the first place, according to this latter conceptualisation, in order to be a democracy it must have the competence to organise free, fair, and regular elections with universal suffrage, free of dominant areas reserved for certain groups - be they military, economic, political, or social. It must be responsible, be accountable to the electorate. Secondly, this responsibility must be both vertical and horizontal. The former allows for control of those being elected by the electorate through elections and the latter is intended to ensure that a watch is kept on those in office - a verification of the actions carried out by the different powers. Thirdly, this concept of democracy has as its point of departure the principle that political and civic pluralism should be guaranteed both at the individual and collective level.

In relation to the latter aspect, it is important to underline its importance, since it includes three propositions which are not normally considered in the traditional definitions of the concept of democracy. First, the demands of political and civic pluralism make it impossible for cultural, religious and other minorities to be denied the opportunity to express their political interests. Next, beyond political parties and elections, citizens have many channels enabling their interests and values to be expressed and represented, channelling their concerns, for example, through a series of groups, movements, or associations. Thirdly, not only are citizens guaranteed the freedom of association and pluralism but, at the same time, there are alternative sources of information. These, for example, ensure that citizens will have access to non-official political information.

Similarly, leading on from these basic definitions, there are intermediate conceptions of democracy which incorporate the civil rights of expression and association but which, however, allow for a considerable restriction of citizens' rights. Equally, there are pseudo-democracies which are regimes with a minimum of democracy - usually they accept the existence of independent opposition parties - but in which the characteristics of authoritarian regimes prevail.

Thus, in Latin America and the Caribbean, in spite of the third wave of democratisation, 'semi-democratic' regimes prevail, which, to a large extent, have distanced themselves from liberal democracy. I believe that the debate between electoral and liberal democracy is one of the fundamental points to be considered in an analysis of the third wave of democratisation. Electoral democracy in the region is 'more and more empty, non-liberal, delegative and downtrodden' (Diamond: 1996, p. 30), widening the gap between liberal democracy and electoral democracy in the region. In the same way, there are more marked trends towards disorder, the violation of human rights, legislative and judicial inefficiency, corruption, impunity and privileges for the military. The role of the United States and the international community has been key in the region in propagating the hegemony of democracy and countries have been obliged to assume electoral democracy as a fundamental prerequisite for receiving the recompense of economic assistance that has been requested.

The current theoretical debate with respect to democratic systems, especially in the region that concerns us, revolves around democratic consolidation. The point of departure is democratic transition or what Samuel Huntington (1996) has called the third wave of democratisation, which appeared in Latin America and the Caribbean at the end of the Eighties, while other democracies in the region came about in the second wave, in the Sixties and Seventies. Generally the idea is that we are moving from a stage of expansion to a stage of consolidating democracy. Likewise, there are new alternatives to democracy: the Islamic alternative and the Asian authoritarianism.

Nevertheless, in this transition towards democracy in this third wave, there is the same concern as with the earlier two waves that, subsequently, these will degenerate in several countries into new forms of authoritarianism. In this way, according to Huntington, historically the transition towards democracy has been accompanied by transitions from democracy towards authoritarianism.

Similarly, according to the academics who study democratisation, there are two schools of thought (Huntington: 1996). First, there are those who believe that there are certain necessary preconditions - economic, cultural and social - needed before a society can become democratic, whereas others believe that democratisation comes about as a result of the ability of certain leaders to facilitate the transition. Huntington argues that both are necessary, notwithstanding indications of erosion of this third wave of democratisation as happened with the earlier two waves. Therefore, it is necessary to consolidate this third wave of democracy, to which end the priority should be the consolidation and not the creation of new democracies.

Furthermore, he argues that the problems facing these new democratic processes are not ideological, but the result of ethnic conflicts, instability and confusion brought about by a multi-polar world and the horrors of ethnic 'cleansing'. In contrast to the earlier wave of democratisation, the current danger is the erosion of democratic systems and not coups d'état. For this reason, in Latin America and the Caribbean the most serious danger is the concentration of power in the Executive, with the reducing or open suspending of Parliaments and the exercise of the aforementioned power by decrees. Therefore, we have the expansion of the so-called authoritarian democracies, 'the agreed strong-men' and 'delegative democracy', all of which instead of strengthening democracy have weakened it.

Thus, Diamond (1996) asks if we have not come to the end of the third wave and postulates that currently the fundamental objective of the actors and institutions throughout the world should be rather to avoid the overturning of this third wave of democratisation, since in practice it seems that the third wave of democratisation is coming to an end. The current context appears to show that the advance of liberal democracy has been stopped, as has political freedom in general, while there is a trend towards retrogression in electoral democracies.

Against this background, pseudo-democracies are being expanded - hollow democracies in which there is only the shell of a democracy. In this way, current processes seem to indicate that we have entered a static period, which could mark the beginning of 'going backwards with the wave'. This retrogression in Latin America and the Caribbean is taking place not only in those countries which were democratised during the third wave, but also in those, such as Venezuela, democratised in the second wave but whose democratic systems have suffered serious setbacks and have been on the decline.

Accordingly, there arises what the author calls 'the imperative need for consolidation'. If we seek to avoid the retrogression - which is impossible in relation to the first two waves - we have inevitably to consolidate our democracies, which can only mean prepare the way for liberal democracy. This process would be attained in harmony with the aspects developed by Diamond, through changes in political culture. Therefore, democratic consolidation would be encouraged basically by institutional, political and behavioural changes.

However, despite the consensus around the fundamental topic of debate being the consolidation of democracy, there are different points of view and a difference of opinion as to what consolidation means and as to how to define a consolidated democracy.This latter debate has as its main exponents, on the one hand, Linz and Stepan (1996) and, on the other, Guillermo O'Donnell (1996 (a)/(b)).

In this debate, Linz and Stepan have argued that there are three necessary minimum preconditions in order to arrive at a democracy that can be considered to be consolidated.These are the presence of the State, the carrying out of competitive and free elections and that those governing do so in a democratic manner. In relation to this last-mentioned precondition, to govern democratically means that it is necessary to respect the Constitution, individual and minority rights, the functions of legislative power and to rule with due regard to a State of Law. In summary, a consolidated democracy would be one which has a political regime in which there is a complex of institutions as well as rules and motivation which are considered to be the only way of governing.

Accordingly, such a definition combines behaviour, attitudes and constitutional dimensions which guarantee that democracy, defined in this way, is the only valid system of governance. Equally, they point out that all this means that a new field or research should be established, namely that of the variety of consolidated democracies.

Similarly, they hold that a consolidated democracy requires much more than elections and markets since there are five conditions which need to be developed to reinforce a functional State.The first of these conditions is that there should be the development of a free and active civil society.The second is that there should also be a relatively autonomous political society.Thirdly, the State and political actors should operate within the rule of law, with the aim of protecting the rights of individuals and the right to free association, for which it is also necessary to have a State bureaucracy. Finally, it is equally necessary that in economic terms the society is institutionalised.

Accordingly, 'a consolidated democracy needs its citizens to develop a positive attitude towards the fundamental institutions of a politically democratic society: political parties, the legislative power, elections, electoral regulations, political leadership and inter-party alliances'. Linz and Stepan:

1996, p. 17) Similarly, the formulation and implementation of mechanisms that make rulers accountable and allow for a State of Law are indispensable. Nevertheless, they make clear that there are two fundamental obstacles standing in the way of consolidating democracies. One of these is ethnic conflict and the other is - in the case of those States that are undergoing economic reform and political reform simultaneously - the disenchantment of the popular sectors in regard to their hopes for economic betterment.

In the selfsame view of indicating the prerequisites for the consolidation of a democracy, Fukuyama (1995) points out that there are four levels at which a democracy should be consolidated. The first of these is on the ideological level, on which there should be a normative ground swell around the need for a democratic system and a market economy. The second level is institutional, wherein we have the Constitution, the judicial and party systems, as well as a market structure. Another level is that of civil society, where spontaneous social structures should be reinforced independently of the State. Finally, at the deepest level, is the cultural prerequisite. For this author a basic issue is the relation between free markets and democracy, in which much stress is placed on civil society and culture, since these will serve as a counterbalance to atomising individualism and the traditional liberal dogma at both the economic and political levels.

Therefore, in confronting the problem of democratic consolidation, the question poses itself: What are the factors which lead to the durability of a democracy? Przeworski, Alvarez, Cheibub and Limongi (1996) try to answer the question, pointing out that it is the existence of a democratic system, well-being, growth with moderate inflation, an increase in equity, and an international climate favourable to Parliamentary institutions. Accordingly, if a democracy is to endure there must be economic growth, which in turn must be underpinned by democratic systems with institutions based on a parliamentary practice. This emphasis on a Parliamentary system, which is also developed by Linz, Valenzuela and other authors, is an extremely important and polemical debating point in the case of the wider Caribbean. For this region provides a significant test case to verify the validity of just such a proposition.

Nevertheless, Guillermo O'Donnell has criticised this concept of consolidated democracies. In the first place, he holds that this concept is based on an incomplete and restricted definition of democracy, which takes up again the Robert Dahl definition of polyarchies. Similarly, he argues that we should consider just as important the informal rules of a political regime and so he shows that Linz and Stepan fail to take into account the problem of clientelism and horizontal responsibility which means that other State organisms control the different State institutions.

In this way, he concludes that the 'illusion' of consolidation has as its basis the fact that democracies which are considered to be consolidated are only those that resemble the model of democracies in the North and that the polyarchies informally institutionalised, amongst which some are in Latin America, are also democratic. His basic criticism is that the democratic model used by Linz and Stepan and other authors, is not necessarily adaptable to other realities.

At the heart of the discussion around democratic consolidation is another bone of contention concerning the fundamental elements which produce the consolidation. These differences of opinion come in three strands which include, on the one hand, the need to develop new political cultures whilst, on the other hand, others give precedence to institutional changes. A third strand has been that which establishes the relationship between structural adjustment and democratic consolidation.

In regard to this last-mentioned strand, Linz (1996) distinguishes between those that establish a 'tightly-coupled' relationship between economic and political reforms and those who present the link as 'loosely-coupled'. The latter hold that there does not necessarily have to be a relationship between economic and political reforms, while the former considers the two necessarily linked. In introducing the variable of the political regime, a tendency has developed to put forward the idea that economic reforms develop better under authoritarian regimes while others argue the need to put forward such reforms within the framework of democratic regimes.

Similarly, it has been pointed out that economic reforms come in two stages: a first phase in which they are applied by a small group of technocrats, usually using the surprise factor, and a second phase which requires more profound institutional reforms needing popular support and so cannot be carried out on the basis of delegative democracy or in an authoritarian manner. Therefore, this second phase requires the building up of political and social consensus on long-term reforms and, in this way, one of the fundamental questions is how to move forward with economic reforms and, at the same time, consolidate democracies. Accordingly, the debate centres on the compatibility or incompatibility of economic and political reforms (Armijo, Biersteker and Lowenthal: 1994).

In relation to this compatibility or incompatibility, Haggard and Kaufman (1994) have pointed out three key topics: the role of the State in arriving at sustained growth, the consequences of the reforms for the distribution of wealth and what this implies in political conflicts as well as for the responsibility in the process of reforms. In this way, the unpopular consequences of the economic reform processes have a negative impact on democratic regimes, causing apathy, social violence, increasing the levels of criminality which can lead to support by both elite and popular groups for authoritarian ways out in order to control economic problems and to seek alternative solutions to these.

The role of political institutions in the consolidation of democracies today is increasingly associated with the relationship between economic and political reforms.Thus it is argued (Haggard and Kaufman: 1994) that economic reforms require the strengthening of civil society and the establishing of an efficient State bureaucracy that can respond to the changes. Likewise, it has been pointed out (Maravall: 1994) that the nature of political institutions is intimately related to the capacity of a democratic system to put forward economic reforms, since it is necessary that a regime has legitimacy and thereby the possibility to build consensus and negotiate: an efficient State. Therefore, currently, economic reforms need a process whereby the State is reshaped.

In light of this argument, we see that it is a reality in Latin America and the Caribbean that the increasing decline of the State has become an important destabilising force. Three factors figure (Naim: 1994) in this deterioration attributable basically to an abandoning of the State. First, in the decade of the Eighties, the need to reduce State expenditure linked to the increasing bad taste left by corruption, squandering and the inefficiency of the State began the deterioration. Secondly, there is the trend towards decentralisation and, thirdly, there is the fact that the establishing and developing of new institutions to support economic reforms is a long, expensive and technically complicated process. After the first phase of reforms - centered on the macro-economy - what is needed is the creation and rehabilitation of institutions, involving the dismantling of the traditional statist model and the construction of a new State, which in turn has to respond to a potentially explosive social situation.

Democracy cannot be conceived of as only a political problem, of the political regime in place, but is also an economic and a social problem. Can there be democracy if there are large sectors of the population that are excluded and marginalised in economic and social terms. ? Do these excluded and marginalised sectors exercise their political rights granted by a democratic regime? Given these questions and in light of the current political, economic and social situation in the wider Caribbean, it is of capital importance to analyse the arguments of O'Donnell with respect to delegative democracy.

This delegative democracy, explained by O'Donnell in a series of publications (1992,1993 and 1994), is enshrined in the need mentioned earlier to look for alternative definitions that accord with the reality we are studying. In effect it would be a proposal as to how to analyse non-consolidated democracies. In this way, the author proposes we distinguish between representative democracy and delegative democracy. In representative democracy, one of the basic differences is the existence of a network of institutionalised powers in the formulation of policies. In the absence of a solid network of institutionalised powers, delegative democracy, by contrast, is based on a history of strongmen (O'Donnell).

The characteristics of this delegative democracy fall into two broad categories: political and economic. There are three political characteristics of this type of non-consolidated democracy. In the first place, power is concentrated around a leader and his cronies, which leads, secondly, to a lack of participation in decision-making by different political, economic, and social institutions. Personalism and authoritarianism prevail. Finally, institutionalisation - already fragile - is further weakened. In the economic sphere, least developed in this proposal, there are two basic characteristics: the application of economic reforms in secret and surprise fashion and a policy of privatisation which directly affects the State.

GOVERNABILITY

In the scant bibliography available on the problems of governability in Latin America, the stress is on the key to the problem of governability being the apparent contradiction between the implementation of a package of neo-liberal policies for structural adjustment and the attempts to reinforce democratic systems, or in the case, for example, of several Central American countries or of Haiti, to democratise. In other words, how to collate the application of structural adjustment, which had led to widening social differentials and increased poverty with maintaining or reinforcing democracy. In the specific case of governability, the key question is: How can changes be made which allow for greater governability, within the framework of the current economic and political crises?

With respect to governability, there seem to be two fundamental ideas which prevail: one of which we will call restricted and the other wider and all-embracing. In general terms, the former has as its basis the relationship between the State and civil society and defines governability as the efficient processing, on the part of the State, of civil society demands and the channelling of conflicts so that these latter do not threaten the stability of the socio-economic and political system.

In this restricted concept, one of the chief aspects is that the interests of civil society are channelled through the State so that governability allows for this relationship between the citizen and the State: there is a constant flow of communication between civil society and the State (Torres-Rivas: 1993). For this reason reference is made to the capacity of the State to attend to and resolve basic problems.

In the same view, another dimension of governability is the efficient exercise of power (Camou: 1993).This dimension is related to who is going to exercise power and with what rules of the game - how it is that power is exercised. In this way, the government relies on the strength of the party political system and a respect for the established rules of the game. In relation to this strength, it is felt that there should be a clear idea of the functions of the parties and the government. Similarly, the society in general, should also be in agreement with these functions and so it should be a widely accepted order.

Likewise, governability has also been addressed in these terms:

to govern a society is nothing but resolving problems through public policies (Malloy, 1992, p. 133). In consequence another important dimension of governability is the principle that political parties are the fundamental channels since the electorate votes them in to represent their interests and make decisions regarding public policies. The problem of governability, therefore, refers to how power is exercised and distributed and how one has access to it.

Governability is also seen as 'the State's capacity to integrate and lead society as a whole' (Maihold: 1995). Democratic governability emphasises participation and civil society establishing consensus. However, the definition of governability is also influenced by different ideological perspectives, essentially conservative, liberal, and Marxist ones (Maihold: 1995).

The conservative perspective believes that problems of governability arise when there is an excessive demand on the State by civil society and that civil society, therefore, needs to be demobilised with the objective of returning to a manageable balance.A neo-conservative vision conceives of a self-regulated society in which the State carries out basically the role of guaranteeing individual rights.The liberal perspective shares, equally, the idea of overload and will argue the need to restrict political action to the limits of the market. However, the Marxist perspective frames the problems of governability in the context of the consequences of the market economy and the crisis of the welfare state. This perspective gives the State a key role in the return to governability since it will act to preserve the interests of private property.

In this way, the crises of governability at the bottom of this restricted concept are analysed with two problem issues: reform of the State to make it more efficient, and to educate its citizens, insofar as the use of legitimate means for channelling their demands are concerned.Therefore, the idea which prevails is that to overcome the crisis of governability there should be technical and administrative efficiency and political will to face up to and resolve, as far as is possible, the problems of poverty and exclusion.

Thus, currently in Latin America, it is argued that the solution to the problems of governability is directly related to how to resolve specific economic problems (Malloy: 1992). In this way the economic crisis absorbs largely the State, which leads to the criticism that there has not been a process of reflection and changes at other levels, thereby weakening the capacity of States to implement policies to face the crisis.

In this way, in a delegative democracy an 'authoritarian style of governability' prevails, in which there is no recourse to negotiation or consultation with other groups, thereby reducing support for its policies. Despite the fact that elections continue to be held, the style of governing will be authoritarian. Since this is the style which predominates, the access of organised civil society to governability is a fundamental problem. As most sectors of society are excluded, there will be less governability. For example, governments, through technocratic policies, have defined the role of the business community, but have not allowed access to this debate. There is no concept of the distribution of power, but rather the idea of concentrating it even more.

Similarly, in this restricted conception of governability in delegative democracies, the executive power is the one which must lead on and administer the economy. Problems arise between the executive and legislative powers since often the latter tries to modify or obstruct the implementation of economic policies or political reforms of the former (Malloy: 1992).

An extension of the concept of the relationship between governability and development emphasises the need for governments to be responsible in the administration of economic and social resources. Governability will be, then, the efficient, efficacious and legitimate exercise of these resources. Here too we have the problem of ungovernability as being 'an excess of actors' that has obliged the government to 'do without the State' (Maihold: 1995 p. 73), to be able to coordinate directly with civil society leaving aside the political parties and Parliaments.

To this a contributory factor is the fact that the parties have functioned essentially as clientelist mechanisms. They have not fulfilled their role as intermediaries between civil society and the government, which has led to problems of governability since the civil society groups have put pressure directly on the executive power. In this way, the executive, in times of crisis, is subjected to pressure not only from civil society but also from the opposition parties and on numerous occasions from actions of its own party.

Thus, the restricted concept of governability is situated basically in the framework of the government's management. Historically (Calderón: 1995) this restricted concept was related to that of political instability, so that, in the mid-70s, authors such as Crozier, Huntington and Watnaki related it to the political crisis. In this relation, ungovernability was a consequence of the incapacity of political systems to process the multiple demands that were the fruit of broader political participation. Governability, in this context, referred to the capacity of the system to process these conflicts.

Claus Offe, at the beginning of the Eighties, argued rather that 'the processes of accumulation, without political regulation produce ungovernability, and in the capitalist regime there would be a tendency towards the inertia of ungovernability' (Calderón: 1995, p. 45) Thus the development of this restricted concept, in the Latin American context, associates it basically with political stability, focusing on governability versus ungovernability, showing the pre-eminence of the notion of governability as the capacity to process demands and to resolve problems.

In contrast to this restricted concept, there emerges an all-embracing concept - social governability. In this relation, Calderón proposes that the analysis of this should include two principal points. First, the effective capacity as well as the authority that the executive power should have against the other powers of the State and society. However, he introduces the idea that governability should include too 'the democratic quality of the government'. In this way, the increase in society's participation in self-rule becomes a necessary condition for governability, defining democratic governability as 'the construction of an institutional, plural, conflictive and open order.' (Calderón, 1995, p. 45).

In this sense, a more all-embracing vision defines governability as the 'capacity of the political system and the society as a whole to make adjustments and innovate to make strategically viable a national project and to process and to respond to the demands of governability' (Ungar: 1993, pp. 10 - 11). According to this definition, there are five basic elements of governability (Ungar: 1993). First, there is the capacity of the rulers - of both public and private institutions and of civil society to put forward initiatives and take decisions as defined objectives.

Accordingly, there should be legitimacy in the sense of minimal consensus and cooperation between the different actors. Thirdly, the government should be capable of controlling conflicts, always respecting the established rules and accepting dissent. Similarly, the evaluation of government administration is fundamental to accountability. Finally, citizens should participate in making and implementing decisions and in the government's administration. Thus governability should be seen from the perspective of the interaction between political, social and economic elements.

Similarly, Luciano Tomassini (Maihold: 1995) has pointed out the need to conceive of governability as something more than an administrative process, and argues the need for it to be regarded as three concentric circles. The first are the public sector and government organisms whose function is to manage the economy. Secondly, there are the organisms of the State - the executive power and the other public powers - and their interrelations, as well as the so-called 'Para-State sector' - private and labour sectors and the Armed Forces, for example.The third circle is composed of the relations between the different actors of civil society, the economy and the market.

Likewise, with respect to the relation between governability and democracy two basic approaches have been developed. There are the so-called 'progressives' who hold that more democracy equals more governability and the 'conservatives' who hold a restricted definition of governability in which the idea prevails that with an increase in authority and centralism there will be more governability. In this respect, in many cases, governability is given priority at the cost of reinforcing democracy and therefore, in order to attain a 'democratic governability' - or to govern democratically - free and equal participation must be collated with the efficiency of the government in achieving 'national objectives' (Camou: 1993).

However, instead of being dichotomous, it should rather be seen as a continuum with two poles: a high degree of governability with low levels of democracy and high levels of democracy with low levels of governability. This means that 'to govern democratically is something quite different to having a democracy.' (Camou: 1993, p. 112).

Nevertheless, it has been pointed out (Ruiz: 1993) that this supposed contradiction between governability and democracy is false, since it depends on the concept of governability that one is using. If governability is thought of in the broadest of terms, as encouraging agreements and widening the participation of different social sectors then there is no contradiction. But if governability is conceived of as a relation of some dictating to others, then obviously there is a contradiction because you are using a restricted concept of governability. This restricted concept is in turn very linked with the characteristics of a delegative democracy.

In conclusion, the alternatives to the problems of governability require, first, a rethinking of the type of democracy and overcoming the delegative model which is not relevant to the current context. Secondly, as a function of this necessary rethinking on the type of model of democracy, it will also be necessary to tackle governability from a more all-embracing vision, taking into account the five elements of governability we have earlier noted.

Thus, Maihold points out that in order to develop democratic governability it is necessary to design strategies for governability. The first of these is the construction of an effective citizenry, aware of its rights and responsibilities. He holds that the natural arena for debate and arriving at consensus is the local arena, hence the need for decentralisation.The second strategy refers to the need to 'redefine the social fabric, the productive culture and working relations' (Maihold: 1995, p. 74) This means a necessary interrelation between social, economic, political and cultural factors. The third strategy should be directed towards the search and formulation of a national project in the long term to establish consensus around the conditions for this and the objectives which are sought. Thus it is fundamental to reinforce the networks and associations of civil society so that they can give a political articulation to this society. It is just as necessary to develop a democratic culture.

However, the construction of social or democratic governability in the wider Caribbean faces not only the challenge of overcoming delegative democracy and a political culture which is also delegative, but also the process of erosion of a statist model or the so-called 'Central-State Matrix' (CSM). The salient characteristics of this model (Cavarozzi: 1991 and 1993) at the economic level were import substitution, closed or semi-closed economies, state control of markets and a 'moderate' inflation. At the political level, this model led to the development of a strong State which claimed to be able to resolve political and economic problems alike, but which, in many cases, led to a hyper-politicisation of the society, despite the fact that the participation of the population was usually reduced to participation in elections.

Running up debts was resorted to, resulting in the debt crisis which, together with changes on the international stage, led to the exhaustion of, or crisis with, the statist model. Generally, this exhausting of the statist model was characterised by an increase in the fiscal crisis, a considerable reduction in private investment - national and foreign - as well as by a notable reduction in international loans and a move towards high levels of inflation.

In the wider Caribbean, at the end of the Seventies and the beginning of the Eighties, this model showed clear signs of being exhausted. The formula used to face up to the crisis was that of opening up economies and efforts to put forward reforms which would lead to a modification in the participation of the State; what was sought was to eliminate the tutelage that the State had exercised hitherto. However, the fundamental problem to be faced was how to carry out this opening up and political reforms without producing problems of governability, due to the new role - considerably reduced - which the State would have.

Similarly, given the negative consequences of adjustment policies, there was a tendency to lay the blame at the door of the political parties and their leaders, causing the disenchantment and isolation of large segments of the population with regard to the parties and the State. Accordingly, different groupings in civil society emerged more strongly.

With this upswing of civil society it has been pointed out that its definition in Latin America (Lecher: 1995) has passed through different stages. The first is a liberal trend which considers that the strengthening of civil society is a mechanism which allows social development to be put forward on the basis of private enterprise. A second trend is communitarian, which believes that the strengthening of civil society will bring about new social movements and the creation of 'solidarity networks' to 'counterbalance market forces'.

Notwithstanding the upswing of civil society, it is thought (Lechner: 1995) that the second trend will face three basic challenges in the coming years because of the new relations it will have to establish with the market, the State, and the democratic political system. The first challenge comes about because the market has reinforced the 'I culture', which means that putting forward community projects is more and more difficult. The second challenge comes about because the relationship between civil society and the State means that there is a multiplicity of players at the heart of civil society necessitating a discussion of the problem of social integration which traditionally had been the role of the State. However, the problem of social integration does not only centre on who will lead on the process, but also on how this will come about in view of the not so democratic relations that have characterised the different models.

The third challenge is perceived to be that of the relationship between civil society and the democratic political system, since market policies have caused uncertainty regarding a definition of democracy. In the context of civil society it is possible to reflect on what is political democracy and the role of civil society in the reconstruction of a social order that will get over the current disintegration and fragmentation. Such a reflection includes what Aguilera (1995) has denoted as 'the politicisation of civil society', which does not mean that the movements in civil society substitute for political parties nor that they turn into political parties but rather that from their position in civil society they have an influence on and participate in political debates and in the process of decision making.

The question arises about the role of civil society in governability or in the crisis of governability. In this regard it is important to get beyond the romantic notion that greater participation by civil society will overcome the problems of governability and that the State and the political parties are exclusively responsible for these problems. The growing fragmentation in civil society could also be considered as a possible source of ungovernability, given that each segment of civil society puts forward its own interests to the detriment of other members of the same civil society. Maihold (1995) has pointed out that one of the fundamental problems is precisely the absence of a national project which enables a coming together of, or a minimum consensus being reached between, the different actors, both political and social. Accordingly, what is produced are 'governability pacts' which allow for divergent interests to be reconciled but not for long-term projects.

Therefore, we are facing what Foley and Edwards (1996) have called 'the paradox of civil society'. In this relation they hold that, irrespective of the definition of civil society, the tendency is to emphasise the positive effects of civil society for governability since it plays the role of pressure group in favour of democracy - often under authoritarian regimes - or it is seen as a counterbalance to the State, thereby guaranteeing democracy. However, civil society may also, due to these functions, turn into an element of ungovernability - herein lies the paradox. A strong civil society that is politically independent may put forward interests that are not necessarily consonant with democracy and governability. Instead of promoting political peace, perhaps an idealistic interpretation, it can also create conflicts that affect the governability of a political system.

PERSPECTIVES FOR DEMOCRATIC CONSOLIDATION AND GOVERNABILITY IN THE WIDER CARIBBEAN

The wider Caribbean in general and the sub-regions within it have constantly debated unity versus Balkanisation. At the national and international level there have been sectors that have promoted respect for differences, insularity, and atomisation at the national and the regional level. The region is characterised by being plural.

The decade of the 1980s has been catalogued as the 'lost' decade for the development of the bulk of the economies in the wider Caribbean. At the level of democratisation and the construction of democratic institutions there was an advance, especially in Central America. However, in other countries of the region - especially those with a long democratic tradition - problems of governability began which, in some cases, endangered the permanence of the democratic system.

Given the exhausting of the statist model in most of the countries of the region from the 1980s onwards, and its economic, political and social consequences, what are the prospects for democracy and its institutions in this decade and in the longer term?

The prospects for the democratic regimes in the insular Caribbean and for those belonging to CARICOM are not encouraging (Payne and Sutton: 1993). In the first place, the viability of the economic development of these countries is in jeopardy, so that they may be obliged to function as 'offshore' appendages to the United States. Secondly, the search for mechanisms of economic growth may produce unsustainable pressures on social stability, which in turn will have repercussions on democratic systems. Thirdly, the growing influence of drug trafficking may lead to levels of corruption which will lead to even more serious problems of ungovernability due to corruption, anarchy and illegality.

In this regard, the economic situation of the 1990s foreshadows problems for the future of the democratic systems and institutions in the Anglophone Caribbean (Domínguez: 1993). These threats derive not only from drug trafficking but also from the exhausting of the statist model. As indicated previously, drug trafficking is considered to be a threat to security, the social structure and political order. Given the growing economic crisis, how can the corruption of politicians and bureaucrats through drug trafficking be dealt with. ? Despite the creation of a regional system of security to combat it, economic limitations raise the question as to how to finance these efforts. In the end, in the whole of the wider Caribbean, drug trafficking brings insecurity and threatens the democracies of the region.

Can the Caribbean maintain its democratic institutions in the face of the exhausting of the CSM? As in most of the region, in the Anglophone Caribbean there is resistance to ending the statist model (Domínguez: 1993). This resistance comes from different sectors of society. For the private sector a change of model would oblige it to compete and lose the privileges of protection which it had with the statist model. At the level of many political leaders, also, resistance is envisaged since to do away with the CSM means to lose the support of a large part of the population. Therefore, in many cases there is the temptation to return to populist and clientelist policies with the aim of maintaining popular support. Lastly, there is the resistance of large sectors of the population because of the economic and social consequences linked to the change of economic model.

In the Anglophone Caribbean there are additional problems (Domínguez: 1993) such as the weakening of the labour unions that had historically been an important support for the political parties and, furthermore, the maintaining or worsening of the ethnic polarisation of the political system in some countries such as Trinidad and Tobago.

In Central America, the decade of the 1980s was characterised by political negotiation in search of peace. The Central American agenda has been focused on peace, reconciliation, democracy and, recently, development within the framework of regional integration. The Esquipulas agreement was premised on the principle that without democracy and peace there can be no development (Arias in Sanchez and Delgado: 1993).

In this regard, with respect to the Central American countries that were democratised in the third wave, Karl (1995) presents the principal arguments, which are debated both in favour of and against the possibility of a consolidation and deepening of democracy in the region. On the one hand, there are those that hold that democracy will be consolidated and deepened, based on the argument that it is not very probable that there will be a retrogression to 'reactionary despots' (Karl: 1995), especially in Nicaragua, Honduras, and Guatemala where they were previously.

An important element for the consolidation of the democratic systems and institutions is that the social forces have been transformed.The traditional alliance between the agricultural oligarchy, the military and external actors has been weakened and popular forces have developed that have an influence on the political system. Equally, due to the weight of these emerging social forces, the political elite cannot ignore them, thereby creating the necessary conditions for negotiation - a fundamental aspect of democracy.

This higher level of competition between the different social forces opens the door to the construction of a new order, establishing new rules of the game which take the struggle for power from the military to the political field of action.The political system would have as a result competitive elections and pacific mobilisation in defence of the interests of the different social sectors.

However, with respect to those recently democratised countries, it is believed that they have fragile structures and institutions, which could be expanded as much as consolidated a process which would be heavily conditioned by the power of the systems to resolve the most pressing problems. In this sense, it is most probable in the medium term that 'hybrid' regimes will be established (or hard-democracies as they have been called in other Latin American countries) which combine both democratic and authoritarian elements. In the Central America context, however, this would be an advance.

Another obstacle against consolidation in these democracies which are a product of the third wave is the fact that the alliance of traditional forces to control the popular sectors has been weakened and there has emerged a 'New Right' and a popular movement both unarmed and divided. Equally, the greater influence of the popular sectors may be problematic if the traditional manner of resolving conflict on the part of the latter with the elite persists, since these elite are not characterised by their use of mechanisms of negotiation and tolerance.

Similarly, in spite of the fact that conflict has moved from the military to the political sphere, the new rules of the game still favour those sectors that were traditionally in coalitions in the past. Added to this, the marked influence of external actors and the deep social and economic inequalities have not disappeared. Beyond this, there are some analysts that hold (Karl: 1995) that the economic policies promoted by the United States and the Bretton Woods institutions threaten to recreate the political and socioeconomic dynamic which led to the civil conflicts in the past.

In this sense, the fundamental obstacles to the consolidation of democracy in Central America (Karl: 1995) are the deep-rooted dependence with respect to the United States, and the economic crisis. With regard to the crisis, it has been estimated that two thirds of the population live in poverty, almost 40% in critical poverty and 23% cannot satisfy their basic needs (Karl: 1995). Equally, the intimate relation between the mainly agriculture-based economy and the political system makes the political systems vulnerable to economic fluctuations (Karl: 1995).

Likewise, the consolidation and reinforcement of the democratic systems and institutions are threatened by the power, considered by many to be a disproportionate, that the military has acquired. The strengthened military still predominate and continue to have a marked influence in Guatemala, Honduras and Nicaragua while they play an important role in El Salvador (Karl: 1995). It is important to take in to account that historic developments have created a culture of repression and passivity which is in no way conducive to a democratic political culture.

Despite the increasing importance of the popular forces, another obstacle may be the thin on the ground participation, that '..revolves around the notion of crisis: crisis with the parties, a depoliticising of the social movements, a distancing of populations with respect to the State, violence, a boycott of elections by the guerrilla, etc.' (Couffignal: 1994, p. 25) The possibility, therefore, of governability and the consolidation and reinforcement of democratic systems and institutions in the Central American region will depend both on domestic factors as well as on international ones.

In the case of the more stable democracies in the wider Caribbean - Colombia, Costa Rica, Mexico, and Venezuela - they have faced in recent years serious problems of governability. The response to these growing problems has been to try to resolve the problems through reforms and above all through decentralisation and electoral reform. However, the development of local power structures has disconcerted the ruling political elite, many of whom have tried again to take over the political space through traditional centralism. Equally, given the emergence and growing importance of new political and social actors there have been attempts to defend or to reconstitute bipartisan systems, as in the case of Costa Rica, Venezuela and Colombia.

Adjustment policies applied throughout the region have had macro-economic success, but their negative effects, above all the increase in poverty and unemployment, have led to an inevitable social crisis. One of the most serious problems is that the neo-liberal policies do not embrace nor debate development. Therefore, the policies are applied but discussion is absent in regard to development projects needed in the region.

Accordingly, since the 1980s, these countries have faced the consequences of the exhausting of the statist model and the application of modernisation policies, accompanied by consequences that have led to problems of ungovernability. However, in spite of the increasing pressure in favour of political reforms which would lead to a broadening of democratic participation on the part of the emerging political and social actors, the ruling political elite have reinforced delegative democracy.

In the bulk of the wider Caribbean, the growing importance of new political and social actors is intimately linked with the traditional political actors losing their capacity to represent - parties, labour unions, professional associations and parliaments. In this sense, it is vital to discuss alternative mechanisms, asking ourselves whether this means the need to search for new models of representation and if these new models should be based at the local level and ensure cooperation between the different political and social actors.

Another key issue for the reform of the current model of delegative democracy in the region is the problem of responsibility. The creation of mechanisms, which permit voters to hold those elected accountable, is considered as a fundamental aspect in overcoming the increasingly authoritarian elements of these democracies.

It is also important to note the relationship which has been developed with respect to civil society. In this sense, the relationship between the political system and civil society - basically the labour unions, civil associations, non-governmental organisations and the Church - in the countries belonging to CARICOM is being developed independently of the State. Therefore, they have assumed the role of counterweight to State power. Moreover, there is a clear delimitation between the political actors and those, for example, non-governmental organisations that have quite a bit of autonomy in civil society with respect to both the State and the political parties.

By contrast, in the G-3 countries and Central America, the development of most organisations in civil society has taken place under State tutelage. Therefore, they do not constitute a counterbalance to State power and, especially in the G-3 countries, there has been the marked influence of political parties on civil society, leading to a lack of autonomy with respect to political parties and, often, to the State.

DEMOCRACY AND GOVERNABILITY: GLOBALISATION AND INTEGRATION

Leis (1996) has pointed out that there are three cultural or civilising trends with globalisation. The first is the homogenising trend, promoted by neo-liberalism, which sees globalisation as a product of modernisation propelled by the market. Currently it is a dominant trend which conceives of homogenisation in the world around Western capitalism, liberal democracy and Western cultural and social values. Equally, it is characterised by being centralising and having a not very democratic view of international relations.

The second trend - nationalist in nature - conceives of the international functioning like sovereign States. In spite of allowing for increasing interdependence, it conceives of international relations in terms of conflictive relations between countries or regions with different, and at times irreconcilable, political and cultural systems.

The final synergic-hierarchical-eclectic trend comes, according to Leis, from civil society. At the heart of this concept the idea of globalisation is developed not as hegemony but in terms of economic, cultural and political diversity and as of finding solutions also to problems through diversity. We should 'establish an order for the double movement of decentralisation and unification... Diversity and unity are guaranteed through the fecundity of global interaction.' (Leis: 1996, p. 53).

However, despite this last perspective on what globalisation could mean, it is evident that currently together with the expansion of free market, it is leading to the depoliticisation of a large part of the population and, therefore, a 'fragmented-global community' is being generated (Leis: 1996).

How can this fragmentation be overcome? It is necessary to democratise international relations and create the basis for of global governability. The growing networks of non-governmental organisations are important for this democratisation - which in the international arena would be making compatible diversity - and for globalisation, especially because it permits those actors traditionally excluded from the international system to participate in it. It is necessary to create democratic models to face up to global challenges. In this sense Leis points out that 'the governability of global problems is intimately associated with the democratic legitimacy of those institutions affected.' (Leis: 1996, p. 49)

With respect to integration, one of the points of debate is the need to go beyond the traditional economic perspective on these processes. Globalisation and regionalisation mean that integration has to be discussed within a political and social framework too, so that as Serrano Pinto (in Sánchez and Delgado: 1993) has pointed out, the necessary framework for integration is that of a sustainable and participatory democracy which respects social justice.

However, integration has been traditionally dominated by a State-centric vision: the integration schema are in the main inter-governmental organisms and, in consequence, they are constructed and function on the back of governments. Nevertheless, as with the national level, this model is entering into crisis because of the increase in the activity and importance of the different representatives of civil society and the networks which are being established in this regard.

This eruption in recent years of non-governmental actors on the regional scene leads to alternative proposals for incorporating the different actors from civil society. These alternatives come with two approaches. On the one hand, there is the incorporation and participation of representatives of civil society in the core of the existing schema for integration. However, this proposal, coming essentially from governments, has not really resulted in their incorporation for the simple reason that what is sought is the maintaining of the centrist-state matrix, preserving the status quo through small concessions to civil society and using it rhetorically.

This centrist-state concept of integration lies in the notion of international regimes which are arrangements constructed by States to coordinate their expectations and organise their activity at the international level with respect to different areas of interest (Kratochwill and Ruggie: 1997). The idea of international governability has been associated with this concept of the existence of international regimes. The fundamental problems to be addressed from this perspective are those of transparency, since this is required in reality and in the expectations of the actors. Also to be addressed is legitimacy, which is the sphere in which there is most disagreement between different international organisms: which are really legitimate and what are the elements which confer legitimacy at the international level? The third element is epistemic, since there is no knowledge or reflection that is passive or automatic.

However, the most telling criticism is that oriented towards the predominance of a centrist-state vision at the core of the concept of international regimes. For this concept completely ignores actors, themes and schema of integration and of cooperation that are not directly related to the State. The State schema for integration are considered to be the only integration mechanisms, arguing the need to link up with these and participate in their structures, since there are no alternative mechanisms or structures. This concept prevails with those who argue the need for the non-State actors, for example different non-governmental organisations, to have mechanisms and decision making within, centrist-State integration mechanisms such as CARICOM, the SICA and, more recently, the ACS.

With respect to the relationship between democracy and integration, they can be seen as two points which may converge. At the national level, there is the need for democracy as a condition of participation in the schema for integration. Thus, democracy is an indispensable prerequisite. Secondly, there is the role of democracy in the creation and consolidation of regional political institutions. Does democracy exist in the PARLACEN, for example? This would happen through the participation of different sectors and the democratisation of decision making. In the schema of integration, is the representation of the economic and political elite such that decision making excludes other sectors of society?

In the face of the obstacles that emerge through this vision which seeks to preserve the statist model, there is an alternative proposal which argues for the need to construct alternative schema, carry out a regional democratisation of integration to incorporate citizens in these processes and to go beyond the restrictions on participation imposed by governments.

Today in Central America two levels of integration can be distinguished. In the first place, there is that level focused on the centrist-State model of integration that has been developed in meetings or summits of the presidents as well as in fora of vice-presidents and ministers. However, in parallel, an alternative form of integration has emerged centered on civil society, which has functioned through the development of joint projects through non-governmental organisations, business people, universities, labour organisations, co-operative and peasant movements.

The economic vision tends also to conceive of integration only as the free interchange of goods and at the Central American level there is concern about this economic approach of the governments' vision for integration. However, integration is not just a technical or economic problem. It is also political, 'whose variables include the observance of public freedoms, the respect of human rights, the solidity of civil society, the trustworthiness of electoral systems and the observance of social justice' (Arias in Sánchez and Delgado: 1993, p. 49). Therefore, at the political level for Central American countries, the key point in regard to this integration is peace at the regional level.

The Central American System for Integration (SICA) is the legal and institutional framework for the economic, political, social and cultural integration of Costa Rica, El Salvador, Nicaragua, Honduras, Panama, and Guatemala (Herrera Cáceres in Sánchez y Delgado: 1993). It was created to encompass all the organs and institutions of the region and it is an organ which coordinates the execution of policies at the regional level. It has a central structure - the meeting of its presidents - which was conceived as a council of ministers comprising an executive committee, on which all the

States are represented, and a general secretary. It has two organs: the Central American Parliament (PARLACEN) and the Central American Law Court. It was established through the Tegucigalpa Protocol that developed in the same way as the Consultative Committee, which allows for private sectors to participate in the preparation and implementation of political decisions.

Thus, in this case integration has been developed through PARLACEN, which was established on the basis of the second Esquipulas agreement. By 1993 PARLACEN comprised Guatemala, Honduras, El Salvador, and Nicaragua. The headquarters is in Guatemala with sub-offices in El Salvador and Honduras. In contrast to PARLATINO, each country has 20 deputies elected through universal suffrage in the different countries. These deputies belong to different political parties and, accordingly, there are ideological differences. Ex-presidents, vice-presidents, or others nominated by the president also participate in the parliamentary sessions.

The PARLACEN is made up of commissions and the fundamental objective is 'an organ for debate, analysis and recommendations on political, economic, social and cultural matters of common interest...' (Mazzine in Sánches and Delgado: 1993, p. 53). For this reason, it is believed in the region that PARLACEN is one of the institutions that enables the solely economic vision of integration to be overcome since it moves integration to where it can be considered from a social and political viewpoint, thereby permitting a space for political discussion around democracy and peace. In light of all this, one of the principal objectives has to be to avoid a return to violence in the region, such that one of the key agenda items is the military. It is important to note that the Parliament has considered the integration of Caribbean countries such as Belize and Panama. However, in the case of Belize there is the problem of the territorial dispute with Guatemala.

PARLACEN is the only body of political integration that is currently functioning in the wider Caribbean. However, insofar as democracy and governability are concerned, an evaluation would need to be done on its functioning to better determine to what extent it reflects and represents the interests and needs of the civil society of the countries which are represented there. Equally, we cannot ignore its official or governmental character, and would have to examine whether, as with its counterparts on the economic level, it too suffers from being state-centric.

In the case of CARICOM, in 1993, the 'Charter of Civil Society for CARICOM: The People's Charter' was presented for approval, laying the base for the participation of civil society in this organ of integration. In this regard, one of the resolutions was to create a climate apt for political participation within the Caribbean Community that would encourage consultation in order to strengthen governability (Charter of Civil Society for CARICOM: p. 7).

However, the clauses that form part of this document are basically oriented towards guaranteeing a series of rights - political, individual, gender, right of expression, among many others - at the level of each of the States comprising CARICOM.

What is striking in the concept of the 'social partners' is that it is restricted to the need of the different social, economic and political actors to arrive at consensus at the national level. Therefore, what is promoted is the participation of social and political actors at the national level, without any mention of participation in the framework of regional integration. In this way, integration is restricted to the governmental level, without arguing the need to create mechanisms to allow for emerging actors to have access to these bodies of integration.

Similarly, the recent creation of the Association of Caribbean States (ACS), allows for the possibility of forming a regional parliament which would be aimed at channelling the representation of its citizens (Serbin: 1994). Its Convention also foresees this relationship, as does that of CARICOM, with 'social partners', among which the different actors of civil society are included. It has even been postulated that in each case the possibility of participating in the deliberations of the Association should be considered (Gill: 1995). However, to date no mechanisms have been put in place to allow for this participation.

This leads us to propose the need for a discussion on democracy and governability at the level of integration in the wider Caribbean. Among the important points to evaluate would be the identification of other alternative bodies for the participation of civil society in integration. In this regard, the fundamental indicators would be those bodies in which effective participation takes place on the part of civil society in the official schema of integration. Another indicator would be those non-state regional organisms that allow for the real participation of civil society and that put forward processes of integration different to those of the government.

The apparent predominance of the statist model in the schema of integration seems to indicate, equally, that there is not a democratisation of the process of integration, but rather that this is subject to delegative democracy, at best, at the regional level. The other alternative to investigate is whether there is in fact a marginalisation of non-state actors in the process of integration. Were this to be the case, are these actors creating their own mechanisms to act regionally? And, is it in their interests or for their survival to act regionally? This latter question arises given the local emphasis with which civil society acts.

Lastly, it is also important to raise the question as to how integration is affected by the exhausting of the statist model, given that the schema for integration are focused on this model. With respect to governability, the question is: What are the fundamental challenges affecting the region?

CONCLUSIONS

With respect to democracy, it is argued that globalisation and integration are leading to 'political homogenisation'. However, this homogenisation is based on a specific democratic model. Is there a consensus around this model? We have seen that at the regional level there is a growing search for mechanisms which would allow for a more participative democracy, to overcome the 'democratic deficit' of the model of representative democracy present at the national and regional level. Also, the effects of globalisation on the political systems of the region are important, taking into account that the political reforms put forward are precisely a result of this process (Serbin: 1997).

Globalisation has also led several analysts to study 'the transnationalisation of criminality', which refers fundamentally to the growing importance and threat of drug trafficking and organised crime. It is important to analyse the consequences that this has on the democratic systems of the region.

The growing economic, political, social and cultural interrelations implied by globalisation, at the national and regional levels leads to the need to reconsider the restricted concept of governability, as well as national and regional governability.

The above leads us to consider the relationship between democracy, integration and regionalisation. The key question is, what is the role of governability and democracy in integration and regionalisation? Some preliminary ideas to respond to this question are, first, the need to discuss mechanisms and institutions in the schema of integration and regionalisation that will allow for regional democratic governability, notably against common threats. In this relation, it is equally important to democratise integration through mechanisms and institutions that will permit the new social and political actors to have greater participation in the existing schema or in the setting up of new organisms for integration which can overcome delegative democracy.

At a more concrete level, it is absolutely necessary to do a study of the reforms which have been executed with the political institutions. For these have been carried out as very practical issues and have not taken into account the necessary reforms to transform the political institutions and bring them up to date. This study would need to formulate alternative proposals. One important factor is the debate with respect to role of the State.

On the one hand, there are those seeking the reduction of the considerable role of the State in society and in the economy. The critics of this position want to return to the old statist model that gives the State the lead role. Are these the only alternatives? Perhaps new concepts and models of the State are needed.

There should also be a democratisation of the processes of integration, creating channels for effective participation for civil society. To what extent are the declarations of the official institutions of integration with respect to this point not mere rhetoric? What channels for effective participation have been created?

Similarly, in situating democracy in the framework of integration and regionalisation in the wider Caribbean, the key question is, what is the role of governability and democracy in integration and regionalisation? Some preliminary ideas to respond to this question are, first, the need to discuss mechanisms and institutions in the schema of regionalisation and integration which enable regional democratic governability, especially in light of common threats. In this relation Duncan (1996) has argued that in order to maintain governability it is necessary to investigate mechanisms that permit links between local government, national government and non-governmental organisations, thereby responding to a vision of governability through interdependence.

To the end of greater governability that would permit democratic systems to be maintained in the wider Caribbean, it would be necessary to analyse the mechanisms and institutions allowing a greater participation of new political and social actors in the processes of integration as well as regionalisation. Lastly, it would advance the development and consolidation of a regional identity, having democracy as a 'common good' (Serbin: 1996).

In conclusion, it is necessary to advance the consolidation of a regional identity, which could have the development of participative democracy as a shared value. However, it is important to consider that integration should have as its starting point, equal recognition and respect for pluralism and diversity. Therefore, a fundamental aspect of this Caribbean identity is respect for and tolerance of diverse identities, or what has been called a new culture of the tolerance of pluralism (Cuevas in Sánchez and Delgado: 1993). In this way diversity becomes a fundamental aspect of unity.

BIBLIOGRAPHY

AGUILERA, Gabriel: 'La politización de la sociedad civil como recurso de la nueva izquierda', Espacios, San José (Costa Rica), No. 4, April/June 1995. pp. 17-20.

ARMIJO, Leslie, Thomas BIERSTEKER and Abraham LOWENTHAL: 'The Problems of Simultaneous Transitions', Journal of Democracy, Baltimore, Vol. 5, No. 4, October 1994. pp. 161-175.

ASOCIACION DE ESTADOS DEL CARIBE: 'Convenio Constitutivo-Asociación de Estados del Caribe', Revista Venezolana de Economía y Ciencias Sociales, Caracas, No. 4, October-December 1995. pp. 190-202.

CALDERON, Fernando: 'Gobernabilidad, competitividad e integración social', Revista de la CEPAL, Santiago, No. 11, December 1995. pp. 43-54.

CAMOU, Antonio: 'Gobernabilidad y democracia en México', Nueva Sociedad - No. 128, Caracas, November-December 1993. pp. 102-119.

CARICOM: Charter of Civil Society for CARICOM: The People's Charter, 1993. pp. 85-111.

CAVAROZZI, Marcelo: Más allá de las transiciones a la democracia en América Latina', Revista de Estudios Políticos, Madrid, No. 74, Centro de Estudios Constitucionales, October-December 1991. pp. 85-111.

CAVAROZZI, Marcelo: 'Transformaciones de la política en la América Latina contemporánea', Análisis Político, Bogotá, No. 19, May-August 1993. pp. 25-38.

COUFFIGNAL, Georges: 'Introducción: Para qué sirve votar en América Latina?',

COUFFIGNAL, Georges (Comp.): Democracias posibles: El desafío latinoamericano, México, Fondo de Cultura Económico, First Edition in Spanish, 1994. pp. 13-35.

CUPITT, Richard, Rodney WHITLOCK and Lynn Williams WHITLOCK: 'The (Im)mortality of International Governmental Organisations', DIEHL, Paul (Ed.): The Politics of Global Governance, Boulder, Lynne Rienner Publishers, 1997. pp. 7-39.

DIAMOND, Larry: 'Is the Third Wave Over?', Journal of Democracy, Baltimore, Vol.7, No. 3, July 1996. pp. 20-37.

DIEHL, Paul: 'Introduction', DIEHL, Paul (Ed.): The Politics of Global Governance, Boulder, Lynne Rienner Publishers, 1997. pp. 1-6 and 25-27.

DOMINGUEZ, Jorge I.: 'The Caribbean Question: Why Has Liberal Democracy (Surprisingly) Flourished?', DOMINGUEZ, Jorge I. et al.: Democracy in the Caribbean: Political, Economic and Social Perspectives, Baltimore, The Johns Hopkins University Press, 1993. pp. 1-25.

DUNCAN, Neville: A New Model of Governance and Community Development, Guatemala City, First Regional Workshop 'Actores Políticos e Integración Regional en el Gran Caribe', SELA/INVESP/CLAIP-IPRA/IRIPAZ, 2nd and 3rd of May 1996. 38 pp.

FOLEY, Michael and Bob EDWARDS: 'The Paradox of Civil Society', Journal of Democracy, Baltimore, Vol.7, No. 3, July 1996. pp. 38-52.

FUKUYAMA, Francia: 'The Primacy of Culture', Journal of Democracy, Baltimore, Vol. 6, No. 1, January 1995. pp. 7-14.

GALLAROTTI, Giulio: 'The Limits of International Organisations: Systematic Failure in the Management of International Relations', DIEHL, Paul (Ed.): The Politics of Global Governance, Boulder, Lynne Rienner Publishers, 1997. pp. 375-414.

GILL, Henry: 'The Association of Caribbean States: Prospects for a "Quantum Leap"', The North-South Agenda, Miami, North-South Centre, University of Miami, No. 11, 1995.

GUNTHER, Richard, P. Nikiforos DIAMANDOUROS and Hans-Jurgen PUHLE: 'O'Donnell's 'Illusions': A Rejoinder', Journal of Democracy, Baltimore, Vol.7, No. 4, October 1996. pp. 151-159.

HAGGARD, Stephan and Robert R. KAUFMAN: 'The Challenge of Consolidation', Journal of Democracy, Baltimore, Vol. 5, No. 4, October 1994. pp. 5-16

HUNTINGTON, Samuel P.: 'Democracy for the Long Haul', Journal of Democracy, Baltimore, Vol.7, No. 2, April 1996. pp. 3-13

JACOBSON, Harold, William RESINGER and Todd MATHERS: 'National Entanglements in International Governmental Organisations', DIEHL, Paul (Ed.): The Politics of Global Governance, Boulder, Lynne Rienner Publishers, 1997. pp. 57-71.

KARL, Terry Lynn: 'The Hybrid Regimes of Central America', Journal of Democracy, Baltimore, John Hopkins University Press, Vol. 6, No. 3, July 1995. pp. 72-86.

LECHNER, Norbert: 'La problemática invocación de la sociedad civil', Espacios, San José (Costa Rica), No. 4, April/June 1995. pp. 4-13.

LEIS, Héctor: 'Globalización y democracía en los 90: Hacia un espacio público transnacional?', Nueva Sociedad, Caracas, No. 142, March/April 1996. pp. 44-54.

LINZ, Juan and Alfred STEPAN: 'Towards Consolidated Democracies', Journal of Democracy, Baltimore, Vol.7, No. 2, April 1996. pp. 14-33.

MAIHOLD, Gunther: 'Gobernabilidad y sociedad civil', Espacios, San José (Costa Rica), No. 2, April/June 1995. pp. 67-77.

MALLOY, James M.: 'El problema de gobernabilidad en Bolivia, Perú y Ecuador', in MAYORGA, René Antonio (Coordinator): Democracía y gobernabilidad, Caracas, Co-edition CEBEM/ILDIS-Bolivia/Editorial Nueva Sociedad, 1992. pp. 131-147.

MARAVALL, José María: 'The Myth of Authoritarian Advantage', Journal of Democracy, Baltimore, Vol. 5, No. 4, October 1994. pp. 17-31.

NAIM, Moisés: 'Latin America: The Second Stage of Reform', Journal of Democracy, Baltimore, Vol. 5, No. 4, October 19994. pp. 32-48.

NELSON, Joan: 'Linkages Between Politics and Economics', Journal of Democracy, Baltimore, Vol. 5, No. 4, October 1994. pp. 49-62.

O'DONNELL, Guillermo: Interview with Jorge Heine, LASA Forum, Vol. XXIII,

No. 2, Summer 1992. pp. 7-9.

O'DONNELL, Guillermo: 'Estado, democracía y cuidadanía', Nueva Sociedad - No. 128, Caracas, November-December 1993. pp. 62-87.

O'DONNELL, Guillermo: 'Delegative Democracy', Journal of Democracy, Washington, DC, January 1994. pp. 55-69.

O'DONNELL, Guillermo: 'Do Economists Know Best?', Journal of Democracy, Baltimore, Vol. 6, No. 1, January 1995. pp. 23-28.

O'DONNELL, Guillermo: 'Illusions About Consolidation', Journal of Democracy, Baltimore, Vol.7, No. 2, April 1996 (a). pp. 34-51.

O'DONNELL: Guillermo: 'Illusions and Conceptual Flaws', Journal of Democracy, Baltimore, Vol.7, No. 4, October 1996 (b). pp. 160-168.

PAYNE, Anthony and Paul SUTTON: 'Introduction: The Contours of Modern Caribbean Politics', PAYNE, Anthony and Paul SUTTON (Eds.): Modern Caribbean Politics, Baltimore, The John Hopkins University Press, 1993. pp. 1-27.

PRZEWORSKI, Adam, Michael ALVAREZ, José Antonio CHEIBUB and Fernando LIMONGI: 'What Makes Democracies Endure?' Journal of Democracy, Baltimore, Vol.7, No. 1, January 1996. pp. 39-55.

SANCHEZ, Olga M. and Jaime DELGADO (Comp.): Una Contribución al Debate: Integración Regional, San José (Costa Rica), Universidad Nacional de Costa Rica/FLACSO, 1993.

SCHMITTER, Philippe: 'More Liberal, Pre-liberal or Post-liberal?', Journal of Democracy, Baltimore, Vol. 6, No. 1, January 1995. pp. 15-22.

SERBIN, Andrés: 'Transnational Relations and Regionalisation in the Caribbean', The Annals of the American Academy of Political and Social Science, London, Vol. 533, 1994.

SERBIN, Andrés: El ocaso de las islas: El Gran Caribe frente a los desafíos globales y regionales, Caracas, Co-Edition INVESP/Nueva Sociedad, 1997.

STRANGE, Susan: 'Cave! Hic Dragones: A Critique of Regime Analysis', DIEHL, Paul (Ed.): The Politics of Global Governance, Boulder, Lynne Rienner Publishers, 1997. pp. 41-55.

TORRES-RIVAS, Edelberto: 'América Latina: gobernabilidad y democracía en sociedades en crisis', Nueva Sociedad - No. 128, Caracas, November-December 1993. pp. 88-101.

UNGAR, Elisabeth (Ed.): Gobernabilidad en Colombia: Retos y desafíos, Bogotá, Departamento de Ciencia Política, Universidad de los Andes, 1993

Getting down to business at the CPDC Forum, Trinidad, July 1995

The role of the Caribbean Congress of Labour and labour in regional integration

Kertist Augustus

Kertist Augustus is the General Secretary of the Caribbean Congress of Labour. He has been a specialist in collective bargaining for several years.

Introduction

The last sixty or so years have seen the political and economic directorate of this region conceive, develop, implement and abandon several initiatives intended to satisfy the objectives of the growth, development and unity of the region.

The CCL and the labour movement within the region have been supportive of many of these initiatives. We have however always held to the view that no initiative would have a chance to succeed unless it is firmly rooted in the concept of a united and single entity.

The Caribbean Congress of Labour has been in the vanguard of the movement to turn that concept into a reality. We were in the forefront of the effort to bring about a Federation of the territories in the region; we supported the initiative for a Caribbean Free Trade Association; but through it all we have held to the truth that this region is a single entity with the same past, a present that shows parallels from country to country and a future which will be meaningful and successful only if the weaknesses of each member within the region are recognised and the strengths are utilised for the common good.

The CCL is therefore happy to keep the debate on the question of the integration process on our front burners.

We in the CCL are unable to say with any confidence that our regional governments are doing the same thing. However, we hope that our governments in the region will replicate the initiative taken by the trade union movement in continuing the dialogue on the process.

HISTORICAL BACKGROUND

The CCL was established in Grenada in September 1960. However discussion to set up a regional labour movement began as early as the 1920s. In 1926, concrete action was taken to establish an umbrella organisation when delegates from Trinidad and Tobago, Suriname and Guyana attended a conference in Guyana at the initiative of Hubert Nathaniel Critchlow. The conference discussed a wide range of issues, including the political and industrial. However, integration and federation were the major issues or themes discussed.

The CCL in its time has witnessed many attempts at Caribbean unity. Examples are the West Indies Federation, 1958-1962; CARIFTA, 1968-1972; the Leeward and Windward Islands Federation, May 1970; the Grenada Declaration, 1971; CARICOM, 1972 to present; the Trinidad Initiative (Trinidad & Tobago, Guyana and Barbados), 1993.

CCL SUPPORTS INTEGRATION

The CCL has always been supportive of the principle of Integration. Therefore when the West Indian Commission met in Barbados at the Dover Convention Centre in May 1991, the CCL re-emphasised its position with the following statement:

> 'The CCL's position on Caribbean integration is that the working person, where he/she understands the meaning of integration, is anxious to have it implemented and to see it work. The CCL is, however, of the view that basic regional relations have been frustrated by far too many taboos, traditions, and insular elements of protectionism. It is therefore mandatory that a programme be mounted to heighten awareness, and to remove prejudices and elements of insularity. For people to participate meaningfully in any facet of change, they must first understand it, relate to it, and have confidence in it.'

The CCL in its presentation to the Heads of Government in St. Kitts in 1991 stated:

> 'The Caribbean Congress of Labour stands by its record of consistency in that, from the inception of our organisation, we have been calling for and indeed promoting the idea of integration through our many functions and activities.
>
> 'In 1990 we suggested that it was opportune for Caribbean

governments to accelerate the integration process in light of what was and is taking place around us such as in Europe 1992; the United States-Canada common market since extended to Mexico and now known as the North American Free Trade Area (NAFTA); and the breakdown of the Uruguay Round of Negotiations.

'We have called for the strengthening of the institutions which could bolster the integration process; yet we were not unmindful of the fact that the earlier attempts at integration failed because of the absence of mass participation in the process. We have since suggested and recommended that in order for the process to take root and be successful, there must be a co-ordinated effort at educating the masses. We are convinced that people will support and be part of the process once they fully understand it, relate to it, have confidence in it and participate meaningfully in it.'

The CCL's support for integration takes many forms, therefore when the Heads of the OECS announced their intention of forging a closer political union, we supported the principle since we saw it as a catalyst for carrying the regional integration movement forward. However, we called for mass discussions involving the governments, opposition parties, trade unions, employers organisations, churches and the other mass institutions operating in the states involved.

We went as far as to suggest some topics for discussion such as:

1. Form of Administration
2. Form of Political Union
3. Nature and Character of the Executive Structures of the Judiciary
4. Form and Function of the Courts
5. Separation of Powers

We called for the establishment of oversight committees to ensure the accountability of elected officials. Such committees would have powers of subpoena and the power to recommend impeachment.

CONCERNS OF LABOUR

The establishment of a single Caribbean through the integration of the region will present concerns, challenges, implications and opportunities for organised labour. Those areas must be analysed and addressed by the movement if it is to survive and contribute to the process of development in an integrated region.

The trade union movement must:

1. insist on due recognition of itself from the beginning. The labour movement must be accorded an integral co-equal part in the whole process of development of the region. The movement must be seen to have an indispensable role in the process of planning and development similar to the role the private sector is perceived as playing in the process.
2. ensure that there is no weakening of the fundamental rights and guarantees enshrined in the various constitutions of member states. In particular, there must be no derogation of the right of freedom of association. We must insist that our governments do not countenance or encourage enterprises which insist on being non-union. Special attention must be directed to export processing zone activities.
3. make it clear that its continued support for the integration process is conditional upon the governments joining and being active in the ILO and upon their commitment to adhere to all the relevant ILO conventions and recommendations for the protection and welfare of workers. Those countries that are not now members of the ILO should be encouraged to join, and every effort will be made by the Caribbean to defeat the proposal which seeks to implement 'Soft Laws' as an alternative to the standard setting machinery of the ILO.
4. stipulate that its continued support for an integrated region is conditional upon the governments enacting legislation which would provide workers with job security, provide post-employment security, and outlaw unfair dismissal and discriminatory employment practices.
5. ensure that the provisions of the various constitutions relating to the Public Service Commission and the Public Service Boards of Appeal are maintained. These tribunals must be seen to be independent and their decisions must be honoured and respected. Our experience suggests that some governments do not like to respect the decisions of such tribunals (Dominica, Jamaica, and Trinidad and Tobago).
6. seek guarantees that our governments will not move away from the practice of free collective bargaining, especially with public service unions. Some governments are seeking to legislate the pay and conditions of work of public servants. The use of the essential service legislation by some governments seems to be an attempt to erode the rights of workers, especially public servants.

7. ensure in an integrated Caribbean the legislation of a Social Charter which would give legislative protection to the workers who are allowed to move freely within the region.
8. spearhead the thrust for legislating the harmonised laws now being discussed by CARICOM.
9. continue its quest for the implementation of the reciprocal arrangement of the social security/national insurance schemes of the region as provided for in the articles of the Chaguaramas Treaty.
10. be the engine for the eventual realisation and institutionalisation of tripartism which, following the economic conference in Trinidad and Tobago in 1991, was agreed upon as the strategy for the way forward.
11. ensure that every effort is made to protect the environment. In that regard we must insist that an environmental audit be carried out prior to the finalisation of any massive developmental project, if only to guarantee for our children aspects of our countries which we now enjoy and which are threatened by developmental projects.
12. ensure that within its ranks are personnel equipped with the skills and ability to monitor government spending and projects to determine if these fall within the priority determinants of our countries, especially when implemented against a request for wage restraint on the part of workers.

The trade union movement will continue its support for an integrated region once it is accepted that workers' organisations will be free to operate and expand; democracy will flourish; and once justice, peace, bread and freedom for our workers and their families are ensured.

ROLE OF LABOUR AND CCL

As has been stated before, the labour movement and the CCL have always been supportive of regional integration. The labour movement in the early days was in the forefront of the fight for the political independence of the islands and will continue the struggle for the integration of the region.

The CCL is strategically placed to play a significant role in the process of integration. We conducted a series of seminars and discussions on the question of the political unity of the OECS and its implications for labour. We have subsequently organised another series of seminars including the more developed and the less developed countries of the region.

We have already stated that for integration to be successful, information to, and education of, the masses are critical. The CCL has two departments which could, and do, play a major role in the process of integration. I refer to the Education Department, which is already functioning in that regard and the Research Department which can assist in researching areas that are critical to the process and others which could impact on the role and function of unions and the labour movement. I submit that the same is true for individual unions which have education and research departments.

One may inquire what gives the labour movement and the CCL the authority to be so involved in the process of integration. I would submit that in the case of the CCL its constitution, and specifically the Aims and Objectives, provide the moral authority for such involvement. The following are the Aims and Objectives of the organisation:

The purpose of the CCL shall be to:

1. Promote the welfare and interest of all affiliated organisations in order to achieve in the Caribbean region the full organisation of all workers;
2. Fight for the recognition of trade union organisations as the legitimate instruments of the working people to achieve their rights;
3. Work for the achievement of the economic, social, educational, cultural and other aspirations of the workers of the Caribbean region;
4. Support and work for the furtherance of the principles of free democratic trade unionism and seek to represent the free trade union movement in all regional agencies as approved by the General Council which exist or may be set up to perform functions affecting the social and economic interests of working people;
5. Undertake and co-ordinate the defence of the free trade unions against any action or campaign aiming at their destruction or at the restriction of their rights or at the infiltration and subjugation of labour organisations by totalitarian or other anti-labour forces;
6. Maintain and develop a regional clearing house of information and research on the problems of trade union organisation, wages and working conditions, labour legislation, collective bargaining and any other matter related to the implementation of the aims of the CCL.

CONCLUSION

The labour movement and the CCL must ensure that the advancements we have made and the fundamental gains we have achieved in our representation of the workers will, at the minimum, be maintained in an integrated region and, wherever possible, improved. Our fundamental freedoms, the respect for human and trade union rights, the recognition of trade unions, the respect for the principle of free collective bargaining, the preservation and protection of the environment, tripartism and the active involvement of women and youth in the must be jealously guarded by the CCL and the labour movement and must never be sacrificed in order to achieve integration.

531 2162

(1) Why the focus now ~~on the~~ mind rather than the body? Is it that they have

(1) run out of medical ideas

(2) been a part of the demedicalized structure. and many people will refuse or don't bother

(3) running out of funds

(4) being sued once too often

60 | 5Q

9/8

35 = 1/2

3 | 12 1/4   15

4

~~(416 222 5955)~~

~~Sociology~~